T0207760

ANSWERS FOR THE FINAL GENERATION

Is the Bible True After All?
A New Look at the Evidence
before Christ Returns.

ARNOLD V PAGE

WESTBOW
PRESS®
A DIVISION OF THOMAS NELSON
& ZONDERVAN

WestBow Press books may be ordered through booksellers or by contacting:

WestBow Press
A Division of Thomas Nelson & Zondervan
1663 Liberty Drive
Bloomington, IN 47403
www.westbowpress.com
1 (866) 928-1240

ISBN: 978-1-9736-3023-4 (sc)
ISBN: 978-1-9736-3022-7 (e)

Library of Congress Control Number: 2018909253

Print information available on the last page.

WestBow Press rev. date: 8/23/2018

PREFACE

My earlier book, *Z: The Final Generation*, raised several questions that seemed to challenge the truth of the Bible. I believe I found answers to them, but it seemed more appropriate to publish them separately.

The famous Victorian preacher Charles Spurgeon once exclaimed, *"Defend the Bible? I would sooner defend a lion!"* I don't view this second book as a defence of the Bible's teaching against the might of modern science. The Bible is not a shield to protect believers from truth. It is a sword with which to attack untruth. Almost all the contradictions between science and the Bible arise because otherwise valid scientific measurements and conclusions are inevitably based on one simple but false assumption, that the origin of the world was not supernatural.

Z: The Final Generation raised further questions unrelated to science that also demanded answers. Why did all Christ's early followers and apparently even Jesus Christ himself believe he would return within their lifetime? Will a self-proclaimed merciful God really consign people who don't believe in him to an eternity of torment in hell? And is earth or heaven a believer's ultimate destiny?

The Bible is a unity. If we don't believe one part of it

then it is very hard really to believe the rest of it. That's why this book is so important. It is seriously important, both for those who already believe in the God of the Bible, and for those who are searching for the truth.

So fasten your seat belt and hang on to your hat. The rollercoaster ride is about to begin!

Acknowledgements

My heartfelt thanks go to my wife, Ann, for her constant encouragement and prayers and for her absolute belief in this project; to John Andrew, Roger Ball, Jerry Wright and others for freely giving their time and expertise to correct and significantly improve what I first wrote; to the editors of the Open Bible Trust for their expert assistance with the chapter on the destiny of the damned (even though they might still not agree with everything I have written!); to Andrea Billen for her patient and clinically thorough proofreading; and finally to all at the WestBow Christian Press for completing the publication of this book.

CONTENTS

LIST OF FIGURES

LIST OF TABLES

NOTE ABOUT SPELLING

British spelling (e.g. 'centre', 'defence', 'favourite', 'judgement', 'sceptical') has been used throughout.

INTRODUCTION

According to the Bible the universe is only about 6000 years old; human beings did not evolve but were created fully formed somewhere in the north of Iran; Jesus Christ said he would return within the lifetime of his first disciples; and apparently a merciful and loving God will consign the wicked to burn everlastingly in hell. How then can anyone believe that the Bible is true?

In particular, can anyone really believe its revelation that life as we know it will come to an end in only a few years' time with the return of Christ to planet Earth? In my book *Z: The Final Generation*, that's what I claimed the Bible tells us.

In this companion book I want to address some questions that I didn't have space to address in that earlier book. I'll start by repeating what I wrote to explain why the universe may really be only a few thousand years old after all. And then we'll look at some other outstanding questions about the truth of the Bible and its teaching about Christ's return.

If you already believe the Bible is true then this book will help you to answer some of the questions that sceptical friends might ask you about it. If you are one of those sceptical friends then I trust that by the time you finish reading you won't be quite as sceptical as you are right now.

1

The Age Of The Universe

Natural or supernatural?

Let me begin by asking you a question. How do you know that everything was not created yesterday? You might reply that it could not have been created yesterday because you can remember things that you did the day before that. You might show me photos of yourself when you were born. Or a photo of your grandfather in a soldier's uniform proposing to your grandmother on Brighton pier at the end of the Second World War. But I asked, how do you know that *everything* was not created yesterday? Everything includes historical evidence and the memories in your mind. If *everything* was created yesterday then all the evidence would still appear to prove that the world was far, far older, yet all the evidence would be wrong. If everything was no more than a day old we simply wouldn't know it.

Naturally I am not really suggesting that everything has existed for only a day. But suppose that the Bible's account of creation is true, I mean literally true. Suppose that God did make the heavens and the earth, trees, plants, animals, fish, birds, insects and the first man and woman in six days as the Bible tells us. And suppose you could go back in a time machine to the seventh day when everything had just been made and was all sparklingly new. All sparklingly new and *real*. If you could part Adam and Eve for a minute and examine Adam you would probably assume he was about 30 years old. But you would be wrong. If you were a dentist you might be able to prove from his teeth that he must be at least 30. But you would still be wrong. If you were a wood scientist you could examine one of the real trees in the Garden of Eden, take a core sample from the trunk, count the number of annual growth rings and conclude that it was perhaps 100 years old. There would be nothing wrong with your conclusion, on the assumption that the tree had grown naturally from seed. But because that assumption would be wrong your conclusion would be wrong. If you were an astronomer and there had been enough room inside the time machine for the necessary instruments, you might be able to determine the distance of some of the stars. You might find one 10,000 light years away and conclude that it must be at least 10,000 years old for there to have been time for its light to reach the Earth. But if it had been made supernaturally only three days previously then even that conclusion would be wrong. It would be wrong because you had *assumed* that the star had been made naturally rather than supernaturally.

Therefore all scientific measurements and deductions that lead to a very old age for the universe should commence with the statement, "Assuming that the universe was not created supernaturally…"

However, in the Bible God consistently tells us that he did make the universe supernaturally. He made it from nothing *by his word*.

God said, "Let there be light", and there was light. (Genesis 1.3)

By the word of the Lord the heavens were made, and all their host by the breath of his mouth. ...Let all the earth fear the Lord, let all the inhabitants of the world stand in awe of him! For he spoke, and it came to be; he commanded, and it stood forth. (Psalm 33.6,8,9)

...the world was created by the word of God, so that what is seen was made out of things which do not appear (literally 'are not seen'). (Hebrews 11.3)

Understanding the supernatural

Some people, even those who believe in a recent creation, will tell you that God would not have created the first tree with a hundred growth rings in it because growth rings would have been formed only if it had grown naturally. But this is to misunderstand what God did. He did not supernaturally create a *supernatural* tree. He supernaturally created a *natural* tree, a tree with roots that went right down into the ground and could only have taken years to develop naturally, a tree with a trunk so wide it must have taken 100 years to grow naturally, a tree with rings that could only have appeared after 100 years of growth, a fully natural tree of which every part was only four days old. It had to be identical in every way with the same kind of tree that grows today, if only to contain the genetic information necessary to produce another normal tree. I don't know much about genetics, but my guess is that it would have been difficult for a tree without growth rings to produce naturally a different kind of tree that had them.

The same argument goes for light from the stars. If God made a real, natural star 10,000 light years away from the Earth and its light did not reach out to the edges of space it would not be a natural star. But it was a natural star, and it was a natural universe that God made, complete in every way, functioning 100% naturally in every respect.

Since, in consequence, so many measurements of the cosmos appear to demonstrate that the universe is much older than the Bible tells us it is, one might ask, "Did God therefore deliberately deceive us?" No, he didn't try to deceive us. What he made appears to be so old because there was no other way he could have made it. A real fully grown man or woman will inevitably appear to be 30 years old or more; a real fully grown oak tree will inevitably appear to be 40 years old or more; and a real fully formed universe has to appear to be billions of years old or it would not be a natural universe. God didn't deliberately try to trick us. There was no other way he could have done it.

2

The Six Days Of Creation

Six literal days

There's no escaping the fact that the first chapter in the Bible says that God made everything in six literal days, not six long undetermined periods of time.

- Verse 5 of Genesis chapter 1 defines its use of the word 'day'. It says, *'God called the light Day, and the darkness he called Night.'* 'Day' is thus defined as the period when it is light, and 'night' when it is dark. If the writer intended the word 'Day' to mean an undetermined period of time' why include the word 'Night'?
- The rest of Genesis chapter 1 defines still more carefully what it meant by the word 'day'. After each day of creation it says, *'And there was evening and there was morning, one day.'* Jews still reckon that each new day begins in the evening at sunset. The writer was evidently explaining in a way that no one could misunderstand that he was talking about six literal 24-hour days.

- When God later gave his people the Ten Commandments he told them to work for six days every week and to rest every seventh day because, he said, that is what he had done when he created the world. If he had really taken billions of years to create the world then he would have been lying to them.
- The same Hebrew word for 'day' used in Genesis chapter 1 occurs in its singular form another 1150 times in the Old Testament. In this form it *never* means a long period of time. To pretend that it means a long period of time only in the first chapter of the Bible is sheer make-believe.

The only reason for believing that the days in Genesis chapter 1 stood for six long periods of time is that most scientists believe the universe took far longer than six days to evolve. But as we've already seen, scientific calculations of the age of the universe are all based on the assumption that it was not created supernaturally. Therefore the only reason not to believe that the world was created in six literal days is that many people believe the world was not created in six literal days!

A strange order of events

Nevertheless, the order in which the first chapter of Genesis tells us that God brought things into existence is difficult to understand from any natural point of view. It tells us that there was first water. (Genesis 1.2,6) It then says that God made everything else in the following order:

Day 1: Light.

Day 2: A 'firmament' called heaven that separated the water above and below it.

Day 3: Dry land and seas, and vegetation of all kinds: plants yielding seed according to their own kinds, and trees bearing fruit in which is their seed, each according to its kind.

Day 4: The sun, moon and stars.

Day 5: Sea creatures and birds.

Day 6: Land creatures and human beings.

It is true that if God had created everything naturally, much of this would be nonsensical. Where did this water come from that he had to separate into two parts? How could there have been light before he made the sun and the other stars to provide it? How could the first day have had a morning and evening before the earth existed?

One day as I was praying a picture came into my mind. It was a picture of a painting, and the painting showed a stream flowing over a waterfall and down into a pool. God showed me that in real life the stream must have come first, for there could be no waterfall without a stream to supply it. And in real life the waterfall must have come before the pool did, for there would have been no water to fill the pool without a waterfall. But the painting was not real life, it was only a picture of real life. So the artist could have painted each part in any order he chose. He could have painted the pool first if he had chosen to. In a sense, he was creating the stream and waterfall and pool supernaturally. So the order in which he painted each part did not have to correspond to their natural order of creation. Indeed, he could have finished the picture by painting the sun, even though the rest of the scene was already in daylight.

Since God created everything supernaturally he could do it in any way and in any order he chose. Perhaps the original water was the canvas or workbench on which he operated. An artist would not consider the canvas as part of his picture, so maybe that's why God didn't include the water in his items of creation.

Nevertheless let's examine the apparent anomalies in the account of creation a little more closely. People who have had near-death experiences of heaven – totally real experiences of being in a heavenly realm while their bodies were clinically dead – such people frequently refer to the dazzling light that seems to permeate everything they look at.

Brad Barrows, for example, had been blind from birth. At the age of eight severe pneumonia stopped his heart beating for four minutes. In his spirit he was taken to a beautiful field with very tall grass and palm trees that he could see! *"There was tremendous light up there,"* he told two researchers some years later. *"It seemed to come from every direction… It seemed like everything, even the grass I had been stepping on, seemed to soak in that light."*[1]

Captain Dale Black, a commercial airline pilot, was taking off in a twin-engined Piper Navajo when it suddenly lost power and crashed into a stone monument. He found himself alive, but suspended in mid-air above his shattered body. Two angels led him to a magnificent city. *"The entire city was bathed in light, an opaque whiteness in which the light was intense but diffused… It didn't shine on things but through*

---

[1] *Mindsight: Near-Death and Out-of-Body Experiences in the Blind.* K.Ring & S.Cooper, Institute of Transpersonal Psychology, 1999.

them. Through the grass. Through the trees. Through the walls. And through the people who were gathered there..."[2]

So does it still seem so unlikely the first thing God said in his week of creation was, *"Let there be light"*? Perhaps the light was simply a manifestation of the energy that he would need to power everything else he made.

What about time? How could there have been a 24-hour day with morning and evening before a rotating earth was created? Before God began his work of physical creation he made both space and time. The phrase 'in the beginning' indicates that the first thing he did was to create time, for without time there could have been no beginning of anything. Therefore it was not the Earth's rotation that defined the length of a day, but it was the length of a day that defined how fast God had to make the Earth rotate in order to complete one rotation in a day.

It is true that the account of separating water above and below the earth with a 'firmament' or 'expanse' called heaven and then gathering the water underneath the firmament into seas in order to expose the dry land seems to describe an earth that is very different to the one we know now. But once again, a supernatural process of creation does not have to bear any direct relationship to the finished product once it is converted into the real thing. My guess is that a parallel situation would be the kind of explanation a mother might give to her four-year-old son who asks how he was made. "I grew you in my tummy" would not be the whole explanation and would not be strictly accurate, but it would be the most that a small boy could understand.

---

[2] *Flight to Heaven.* Dale Black, Bethany House Publishers, May 2010.

If all this still doesn't satisfy you I've provided an original and radically different explanation of God's six days of creation in Annex 1. It may be of interest to more scientifically minded readers.

In Genesis 2.7 it says, '*…the Lord God formed man of dust from the ground, and breathed into his nostrils the breath of life; and man became a living being.*' God created the first man supernaturally, but only when he was complete did he become a living, natural, human being. This suggests to me that the Lord first created everything supernaturally in ways beyond our natural understanding, and then, when everything was ready, when he was satisfied that the picture he had painted so to speak was complete, he brought it all to natural life by the power of his Spirit. From that moment onwards it functioned naturally.

3

The Universal Flood

The Bible's account

> *In the six hundredth year of Noah's life, in the second month, on the seventeenth day of the month, on that day all the fountains of the great deep burst forth, and the windows of the heavens were opened. And rain fell upon the earth forty days and forty nights … And the waters prevailed so mightily upon the earth that all the high mountains under the whole heaven were covered; the waters prevailed above the mountains, covering them fifteen cubits deep. And all flesh died… everything on the dry land in whose nostrils was the breath of life died. … Only Noah was left, and those that were with him in the ark.*
> (From Genesis 7.11-24)

Whole books have been written on this subject, both for and against the belief that such a universal flood really occurred. I can hardly enter into such a huge debate at this point. But since Jesus clearly believed that the Flood occurred and that Noah built the ark as described (Matthew 24.37-39) I'll content myself with just a few points which I hope cannot be contradicted in support of the account in Genesis.

The Genesis Flood

The Genesis Flood, written by John Whitcomb and Henry Morris back in 1961, was the first book to address seriously the conflict between the Bible's account of the Flood and generally accepted science. It was republished in 2012 as a fiftieth anniversary edition,[3] so it must still have some value. One of the few unbiased reviewers of the book on Amazon said it provides an excellent summary of the creationist standpoint on the subject of the Flood. Here are just five of the points that the authors make, in slightly simplified form:

(i) If all the water in our present atmosphere were suddenly precipitated, it would cover the ground to an average depth of less than 2 inches (5cm). A global rainfall continuing for 40 days would have required a completely different mechanism for its production than what is available at the present day. However Genesis 1.7 speaks of 'the waters that were above the firmament'. If prior to the Flood there was a high-altitude canopy of water vapour free from the particles that are a necessary precursor to precipitation as water droplets, the

---

[3] *The Genesis Flood, The Biblical Record and its Scientific Implications, 50ᵗʰ Anniversary Edition.* J.C.Whitcomb & H.M.Morris, Presbyterian and Reformed, 2012.

resulting increased absorption of the sun's radiation and the more uniform distribution of the resulting heat would have produced a uniformly warm temperature over the Earth prior to the Flood. This would explain the widespread existence of fossils of temperate and semi-tropical plants and animals even near the poles.[4] It could also explain why Genesis tells us that it did not rain until after the Flood. (Genesis 2.5,6; 7.12) Today the temperature in the thermosphere 80 miles above the Earth is very high, conducive to retaining large amounts of water vapour, and water vapour is lighter than air so the existence of such a water vapour canopy prior to the Flood seems perfectly possible.

If water then covered the whole earth to a depth of 'fifteen cubits above the mountains' where did it go when the flood subsided? Psalm 104.6-9 answers the question. It describes how God reshaped the earth's surface after the Flood, raising what had previously been relatively low mountains and sinking what had previously been relatively shallow valleys:

> *Thou didst cover* [the earth] *with the deep as with a garment; the waters stood*

---

[4] '*The general distribution and character of the rocks and their fossil content point to more uniform climatic conditions that those of today. Fossils in the Arctic Silurian rocks are not essentially different from those of low latitudes.*' W.J.Miller: *An Introduction to Historical Geology,* 6th edition, Van Nostrand, 1952, p.116. Similar statements made in geological textbooks about the Miocene, Cambrian, Ordovician, Devonian and Carboniferous eras are quoted in *The Genesis Flood,* cited above.

> *above the mountains. At thy rebuke they*
> *fled; at the sound of thy thunder they took*
> *to flight. The mountains rose, the valleys*
> *sank down to the place which thou didst*
> *appoint for them. Thou didst set a bound*
> *which they should not pass, so that they*
> *might not again cover the earth.*

There is plenty of evidence from fossil finds and echo-sounding equipment that both these events actually happened.[5] Canyons deep below the surface of the ocean, but presumably originally carved out by rivers above the ground, occur all over the world.[6] Near the mouth of the Hudson River they are nearly 3 miles below the surface.[7]

The psalm also makes it easier to understand how all the mountains could have been covered with water during the Flood: they were not nearly so high as they are now.

(ii) A universal flood offers a credible explanation for the formation of sedimentary rocks. Sedimentary

---

[5] Fossils of whales and other sea creatures have been found high in the mountains of Chile and California. In 2015 oil prospectors using echo-sounding equipment discovered a 1.2-mile deep landscape in the North Atlantic west of the Orkney-Shetland Islands, with peaks that once belonged to mountains and eight major rivers. Researcher Nicky White, from University of Cambridge, said: *"It looks for all the world like a map of a bit of a country onshore." Lost world: Ancient submerged landscape of mountains and riverbeds found on the Atlantic seabed.* Daily Mail, July 2011.

[6] *Submarine Geology.* F.P.Shepard, Harpers New York, 1948.

[7] *Principles of Geomorphology.* W.D.Thornbury, Wiley, 1954.

rocks are rocks which have been deposited as sediments, which the *Oxford Universal Dictionary on Historical Principles* defined as 'earthy or detrital matter deposited by aqueous agency'. Obviously these great masses of sediments must first have been eroded from some previous location, transported, and then deposited, perhaps on more than one occasion – exactly the sort of thing which occurs in any flood and must have occurred on a uniquely grand scale during the great flood of Genesis.

(iii) A universal flood offers the best explanation of how fossils were formed. In general fossils are found only in sedimentary rocks. (You can't insert a mammoth into a block of granite.) Tens of thousands of extinct animals, many of them mammoths, have been found preserved whole, with even flesh and hair intact, particularly in Siberia. This could only have happened without their decaying or being eaten by scavengers if they were buried suddenly in the sediments they have been found in.[8] Similarly the fossilization of many kinds of fish is indicative of very rapid burial and solidification, for in normal circumstances a dead fish is eaten by other fish or sea creatures.[9]

---

[8] See for example the Wikipedia entry, 'Fossils of the Burgess Shale'.

[9] '*Several gar-pike, ranging in size from 4 to 6 feet, have been disentombed, as have birds of about the size of the domestic chicken and resembling the snipe or plover in general conformation. In addition, specimens of sunfish, rasp-tongues, deep sea bass, chubs, pickerel and herring have been found, not to mention mollusca, crustaceans, birds, turtles, mammals and many varieties of insects.*' Deposits found

(iv) In particular a sudden universal flood offers the most rational explanation for the extinction of the dinosaurs. In August 2017 the *Guardian* newspaper reported the findings of a paper published by the Royal Society about an unusual dinosaur called the Chilesaurus.[10] The *Guardian* article explained:

> *Dinosaurs were the monarchs of Earth for 160 million years until a space rock collided with the planet 65.5m years ago and wiped out those confined to land. Ornithischia thrived for more than 100 million years, but were wiped out when the rogue rock smashed into what today is the Yucatan peninsula in Mexico. The impact probably created a massive firestorm followed by a decades-long winter that destroyed vegetation, the starting point in the dinosaurs' food chain.*

Quite apart from the extraordinary notion that a rock falling in Mexico could wipe out dinosaurs all over the earth by destroying the starting point of their food chain and presumably all the intermediate life forms at the same time, the scientific paper that the article was supposedly reporting said nothing of the sort. The explanation of the dinosaurs' extinction was pure fiction, made to sound like fact

---

in Lincoln County, Wyoming, described in '*Fishing for Fossils*', Compressed Air Magazine, Volume 63, March 1958, p.24.
[10] *A dinosaur missing link? Chilesaurus and the early evolution of ornithischian dinosaurs.* M.G.Baron & P.M.Barrett, Biology Letters, The Royal Society, 16 August 2017. DOI: 10.1098/rsbl.2017.0220.

in the context of a genuine scientific paper. Many of the 'facts' that we are told emanate not from scientists but from journalists writing for attention-seeking editors.

(v) A universal flood perfectly explains the most common order of fossilized life forms found in the standard geologic column. When the fountains of the deep broke up and the heavens above broke open, the first creatures to be affected would have been sea creatures. Invertebrate sea creatures (molluscs, etc.) would have been buried first in the tide of debris and mud that swept into the shallow seas, then vertebrates (fish etc.) would have been buried, after they had tried to swim to safety. Then, as the flood waters filled the lower-lying land, amphibians would have been trapped, then the slower moving reptiles, then animals (which could initially have escaped to higher ground), and finally birds, which presumably flew around until they died of hunger. This also explains why trilobites, for example, are never found in the same layer as dinosaurs.

The fountains of the deep

The one aspect of the Flood that the authors of *The Genesis Flood* don't seem to have addressed is this matter of the 'fountains of the great deep'. The phrase suggests that vast quantities of water were previously trapped under pressure beneath the surface of the earth and burst out. That is certainly what Walter Brown believes,[11] although much of what he says has been strongly refuted by people who don't believe the Biblical account.[12] However scientists working with the Hubble Space Telescope in 2016 excitedly reported observations which strongly supported the possibility of water being trapped under pressure below the surface of a planet. They identified fountains of water or ice spewing 100 miles into space from the surface of Europa, one of Jupiter's moons. A report on *USA Today* stated, '*Water from this salty sea presumably shoots up through cracks in the outer coating of ice, which measures tens of miles thick or more.*' NASA's Curtis Niebur admitted they didn't have a full explanation for the process. *"We're seeing* [the plumes] *using a completely different technique. That gives you a lot more evidence that it's not just a fluke, that it's actually something physical."*[13]

Even on the earth today geysers of water such as 'Old Faithful' in the Yellowstone National Park continue to spout water into the air; oil spurts out of the ground when it is released; and volcanoes can eject ash 20 miles upwards into the sky. If water was once trapped beneath the earth's crust and was superheated by volcanic magma the generated pressure could well have been explosive.

---

[11] *In the Beginning: Compelling Evidence for Creation and the Flood.* W.Brown, Center for Scientific Creation, August 2008.

[12] *Walter Brown's "Hydroplate" Flood Model Doesn't Hold Water.* G.J.Kuban, http://paleo.cc/ce/wbrown.htm, viewed August 2016.

[13] *Scientists find incredible fountains shooting from Jupiter's moon.* T.Watson, *USA TODAY*, September 26, 2016

A universal belief

Ancient cultures all over the world have independently handed down a story about a great flood that once took place. Wikipedia's entry 'List of flood myths' lists 38 such stories from China and the Far East, India and the Middle East, Europe, North and South America, Africa and even Polynesia and Hawaii. Why is there such a universal belief in a universal flood if such a flood never occurred? Here's one such story from the Philippines. It can hardly have been based on the Biblical story, yet it has elements that clearly match the Biblical account:

> *Once upon a time, when the world was flat and there were no mountains, there lived two brothers, sons of Lumawig, the Great Spirit. The brothers were fond of hunting, and since no mountains had formed there was no good place to catch wild pig and deer. The older brother said: "Let us cause water to flow over all the world and cover it, and then mountains will rise up."*

Here are two more stories. An ancient Celtic myth from Wales tells of a great flood caused by the monster Afanc who dwelt in Llyn Llion, which was possibly Bala Lake. All humans were drowned except Dwyfan and Dwyfach. They escaped in a huge mastless boat or ark called *Nefyd Naf Neifion*, on which they carried two of every living kind. From Dwyfan and Dwyfach all the island of Prydain (Britain) was repopulated.

In Inca mythology the creator god, Viracocha, arose out of Lake Titicaca and made mankind by breathing into stones. His first creations were brainless giants who displeased him, so he destroyed them with a flood and made better people from smaller stones.

Once again, why would people all over the world who had no contact with the Bible believe that there had once been a universal flood if it never occurred? All these myths have some similarities to the Biblical account, yet none of them seems quite so rational. In my opinion the only 'myth' that the Wikipedia article should not have included in its list is the Biblical account of what actually happened.

4

The Age Of Rocks

Radioactive dating

According to the Hebrew 'Masoretic' text, on which virtually all translations of the Old Testament are based, the Flood occurred around 2300 BC and the world is currently around 6000 years old. On the other hand radioactive dating techniques suggest that the earth's rocks are up to 4 billion years old. One or the other is wrong!

The age of rocks is determined using radioactive chemical elements. A radioactive element emits radiation in the form of atomic particles, and in doing so it gradually changes into another element. The rates at which the various radioactive elements change into other elements can be measured. Uranium, for example, very slowly turns into lead. A given weight of uranium will lose half its weight in 4.46 billion years. (I did say it changed very slowly!) The figure of 4.46 billion years is called its half-life. So if a rock has 1gm of uranium in it when it is first formed then 4.46 billion years later it will have only 0.5gm of uranium in it but there will be perhaps 0.5gm of lead as well. (I don't know whether you get exactly 0.5gm of lead from 0.5gm of uranium but you get the idea.)

From the measured proportions of uranium and lead in a rock it is therefore possible to calculate how long the uranium has been there and hence how old the rock is. For example, if there are equal amounts of uranium and lead then half the uranium must have turned into lead so the rock must be 4.46 billion years old. That's the theory as I understand it.

Behold, I make all things old!

When I learned how radioactive dating worked my first thought was, "How does a geologist know that there wasn't already some lead in the rock to start with?" Geologists are aware of this and other difficulties, so they try to get over them by various means.[14,15] However, if God made everything supernaturally then the entire basis of radiometric dating falls apart. God could have created rocks having radioactive elements and the stable elements into which they decay in any proportion he liked.

When I had my house extension built I specified used tiles to match the existing ones. Anyone looking at the extension would assume it had been built at the same time as the main house, not 50 years later. There could be various

---

[14] *Nuclear Processes in Geologic Settings: Interpretation of lead isotope abundances.* R.D.Russell, National Academy of Science, National Research Council publication 400, 1956, pp.68-78.

[15] *Nuclear Processes in Geologic Settings: Leakage of uranium and lead and the measurement of geological time.* F.E.Wickman, National Academy of Science, National Research Council publication 400, 1956, pp.62-67.

reasons why God might have made 'mature' rocks rather than brand new ones. When he made Adam and Eve he could not make two newborn babies and leave them to fend for themselves: he had to make a mature man and woman. When he made fruit trees he could not make tiny first-year saplings or Adam and Eve would have had no fruit to eat for several years: he had to make mature fruit trees. When he made the stars he could not make 'new' ones which had only just started to shine, or Adam and Eve would have died before they could see the more distant ones: he had to make 'mature' stars that had apparently been shining for a long time. So when he made rocks it might have been equally necessary for him to make mature rocks that had every appearance of age, rather than brand new ones. What scientific law states that he had to make a rock with uranium in it but no lead, or one with samarium in it but no neodymium, or one with rubidium in it but no strontium?

In *Z: The Final Generation* I explained why the physical universe and terrestrial life could have come into existence only supernaturally. If the earth's rocks were created supernaturally then radioactive dating will be unable to determine their age, because the proportions of radioactive elements and non-radioactive elements that were in them when they were created will be unknown. And since it is impossible to prove from any observations or measurements whether this natural earth was created naturally or supernaturally, it is impossible to prove from measurements of radioactivity whether rocks really are old or not. The apparent ages of rocks determined by radioactive dating are no proof that the earth is a day older than the Bible implies.

5

The Fossil Record

Radioactive carbon dating

Radioactive carbon (C_{14}) is extensively used to determine the age of things that once lived, so in theory it should be possible to determine the age of fossils by radiocarbon dating. This is how it works. High-energy cosmic radiation from the sun continually changes nitrogen atoms in the upper atmosphere into radioactive carbon atoms.[16] These combine with atmospheric oxygen to form radioactive carbon dioxide. Plants absorb the resulting mixture of normal carbon dioxide and radioactive carbon dioxide from the air and use it to build their cells. Living creatures then eat the plants and absorb the carbon. As a result, a tiny proportion (something like one part per trillion) of

---

[16] A cosmic ray in the form of a high-energy proton (a positively charged particle) collides with an atom in the atmosphere converting one of its neutrons into a separate high-energy ('thermal') neutron. This in turn collides with a nitrogen atom in the atmosphere, replacing a proton and converting it to radioactive carbon. (N_{14} (7 protons + 7 neutrons) + 1 thermal neutron $\rightarrow$ C_{14} (6 protons + 8 neutrons) + 1 proton)

the carbon in all living things is radioactive, the same proportion as the radioactive carbon in the air. You are slightly radioactive!

When a plant or animal dies it stops absorbing carbon from the air but the radioactive carbon already in it continues to decay at a known rate. So from its known half-life of about 5730 years, the relative amount of radioactive carbon that remains in a fossil, mummy, gatepost, or dress made from natural fibres can be used to determine how old it is. For example, if the proportion of radioactive carbon in the carbon content is only half what it is in the atmosphere then the object is 5730 years old or thereabouts, always assuming that the proportion of C_{14} in the atmosphere has remained fairly constant throughout that period.[17]

However, while radiocarbon dating has been used with reasonable success on items from Egyptian tombs known to be around 4700 years old it is not used on fossils for the simple reason that the relative quantities of C_{14} remaining in them are too small to be measured accurately. Of course this is put down to the fact that fossils must be extremely old. In fact the oldest fossils are believed to be about 3.5 billion

---

[17] The historical proportions of C_{14} in the atmosphere have been measured from the rings of ancient trees. Carbon in a tree trunk is absorbed only in the outer ring each year, so each tree ring gives an estimate of the proportion of C_{14} in the atmosphere in the year it grew, after an allowance has been made for radioactive decay corresponding to its age. In recent history the widespread burning of fossil fuels reduced the proportion of C_{14} in the atmosphere, and the atmospheric nuclear tests conducted in the 1950s and 1960s almost doubled it for a while. Claims that trees can provide reliable data going back 13,900 years seem very dubious to me.

years old. But does the near absence of C_{14} in fossils really prove that they are extremely old?

Peter's prediction

In my youth I visited the caves in Cheddar Gorge in Somerset. In one place a cluster of small white stalactites, illuminated by imaginative lighting, was silently reflected in a black pool of water beneath them that looked for all the world like some stunningly beautiful Tolkienian city. In another place a guide told us that a massive stalactite suspended above the passageway and still dripping water from its tip was so many thousands of years old. I asked her how she knew its age. She explained that its rate of growth had been measured over several years so it was possible to calculate when it first began to form from its current size. The question that immediately came to my mind was "How do they know that it always grew at the same rate?" I was not confident enough at that age to ask her, but it did seem to me that in earlier centuries or millennia the watercourse on the surface might have changed direction, or the mineral content of the water might have changed. A similar question could justifiably be asked about the apparent age of fossils when an attempt is made to date them from their C_{14} content. How does one know that C_{14} has always been present in the atmosphere in similar amounts?

If the Biblical account of the Flood is correct and prior to the Flood there was a vast amount of water above the earth, presumably as water vapour, it could and probably would have shielded atmospheric nitrogen from cosmic rays. This would have prevented the production of C_{14}, either in part or entirely, so that anything living before the Flood would have absorbed little or no C_{14}. Therefore every living thing fossilized as a result of the Flood would inevitably have appeared to be far, far older than it really is.[18] The presence of 'the waters which were above the firmament' mentioned in Genesis chapter 1 destroys the validity of radiocarbon dating when it is applied to fossils created by the Flood, and to anything that grew in the years immediately after the Flood while C_{14} levels in the atmosphere began to build up. And if it was the Flood that buried all the now fossilized plants and animals, the apparent great age of fossils determined by measurements of C_{14} cannot be presented as proof that the earth is a day older than the Bible indicates it is.[19]

Nearly 2000 years ago the apostle Peter wrote, '*… scoffers will come in the last days… saying, "…all things have*

---

[18] Coal, which is fossilized wood, contains variable amounts of C_{14}, which are normally explained as originating from the radioactive decay of the uranium-thorium isotope series that is naturally found in rocks. Since some coal has no measurable C_{14} I wonder whether all the C_{14} detected in other fossils comes not from the absorption of C_{14} while they were alive before the Flood but from contamination by other radioactive elements in the surrounding rock.

[19] It is true that a paper published in 1986 by Linick and others in the journal *Radiocarbon* reported that radiocarbon ages were consistently found to be only 15% less than the ages of samples of dead bristlecone pine trees dated back to 6554 BC, but the methods used to date ancient bristlecone pine trees are based on a false assumption, as will be explained later. It is also claimed that radiocarbon dating can be verified 45,000 years back by checking its results against the known dates of cave formations called speleothems, but these 'known' dates were derived by uranium-thorium radioactivity measurements which are also based on a false assumption, as explained previously.

continued as they were from the beginning of creation." They deliberately ignore this fact, that… the world that then existed was deluged with water and perished.' (2 Peter 3.3-6) It's almost as though Peter foresaw how scientists today would ignore the effect of the Flood on radiocarbon dating!

Determining the age of fossils from the geological column

As I explained earlier, C_{14} is not used to determine the age of fossils because too little radioactive carbon remains in them to obtain a reliable value. So how do scientists know, or think they know, how many years ago a dinosaur or trilobite lived? If you are very bright you might guess that they measure instead the age of the rock in which the fossil is embedded, using one of the other kinds of radioactivity I mentioned earlier. But they can't do that because fossils are almost always found in sedimentary rock – rock that has been laid down by sand and mud sediments washed down by water – and sedimentary rock doesn't contain any radioactive elements that might be used to date it. So how on earth is the age of a fossil known? The answer is, it isn't! Let me explain…

Most people are probably familiar with the geological column that appears in school textbooks and reference books all over the world.[20] A simplified American version of this is shown in Figure 1. (The original diagram is public domain from the US National Park Service.)

---

[20] At the time of writing the web page creationwiki.org/ Geological_column has a good explanation of the geological column.

Figure 1: The geological column, simplified

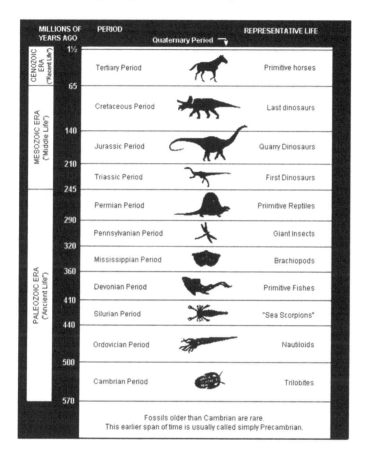

MILLIONS OF YEARS AGO	PERIOD		REPRESENTATIVE LIFE
		Quaternary Period →	
CENOZOIC ERA ("Recent Life") 1½	Tertiary Period		Primitive horses
65			
MESOZOIC ERA ("Middle Life")	Cretaceous Period		Last dinosaurs
140	Jurassic Period		Quarry Dinosaurs
210	Triassic Period		First Dinosaurs
245	Permian Period		Priimitive Reptiles
290	Pennsylvanian Period		Giant Insects
320	Mississippian Period		Brachiopods
PALEOZOIC ERA ("Ancient Life") 360	Devonian Period		Primitive Fishes
410	Silurian Period		"Sea Scorpions"
440	Ordovician Period		Nautiloids
500	Cambrian Period		Trilobites
570			

Fossils older than Cambrian are rare.
This earlier span of time is usually called simply Precambrian.

I had always assumed, as perhaps other people do, that words like 'Cretaceous', 'Devonian' and 'Cambrian' applied to different kinds of rock, and that it was somehow known how old these rocks were, and therefore how old the fossils in them were. But it's nothing like that. The different strata of rock are simply named after the places where the corresponding kinds of fossils were first found, and the ages assigned to the rocks are assigned from the assumed ages of the fossils.

In the early 1800s the English canal builder William Smith noticed that similar fossils were generally found in the same kind of strata throughout England, and that the different kinds of strata were generally found in the same sequence. He also noticed that smaller and less complex fossils tended to be found in lower layers, and larger and more complex organic remains in the higher layers. It was assumed that the lower layers had been laid down first and that therefore the fossils in them were older than the ones in higher layers. Secondly, on the assumption that the theory of evolution was true, it was concluded that many millions of years must have elapsed between the formation of each layer to give time for the successive stages of evolution to take place. Eventually, by measuring radiometrically the ages of adjacent layers of non-sedimentary rocks, some supposedly more accurate timescales were assigned to the various periods of time.

In order to compare rock strata in various parts of the world, a system of 'index fossils' was then set up to identify each stratum. An index fossil is a type of fossil that is easily identifiable and reasonably plentiful.[21] Furthermore it is a fossil that occurs in only one layer of rock at any particular location. That implies that it didn't come into existence before that layer was formed, and that it went out of existence before the layer above it was formed, once again on the assumption that the theory of evolution is a fact. Having assigned a set of index fossils to each assumed

---

[21] Corals, graptolites, brachiopods, trilobites, and echinoids (sea urchins) are examples of index fossils.

period of the Earth's age, they were then used to identify similar rock strata in other geological sites around the world and to assign the corresponding ages to them.[22] Whenever a new kind of fossil is discovered now, it is immediately dated from the age that has been assigned to the rock stratum in which it is found. Thus to some extent fossils are used to date rocks and the rocks are then used to date fossils![23]

The result of all this is the geological column, which many scientists and most of the public now accept as a fact. So why did I say that the ages of fossils are not known?

Unprovable assumptions

In the first place the construction of the geological column is based on unprovable assumptions.

The idea that the lower strata in a rock formation must have been laid down millions of years before the higher strata is based on the assumptions that the theory of evolution is true and that there was never a universal flood. However no one has been able to produce any evidence of evolution

---

[22] *Fossil Frustrations.* D.V.Ager, New Scientist, Vol. 100, 10 November 1983, p. 425. '*Ever since William Smith at the beginning of the 19th century, fossils have been and still are the best and most accurate method of dating and correlating the rocks in which they occur. ... Apart from very 'modern' examples, which are really archaeology, I can think of no cases of radioactive decay being used to date fossils.*'

[23] *Pragmatism Versus Materialism in Stratigraphy.* J.E.O'Rourke, American Journal of Science, Vol. 276, January 1976, p. 47. '*The intelligent layman has long suspected circular reasoning in the use of rocks to date fossils and fossils to date rocks. The geologist has never bothered to think of a good reply, feeling that explanations are not worth the trouble as long as the work brings results. This is supposed to be hard-headed pragmatism.*'

taking place, and a universal flood provides an obvious explanation for the most common sequence of fossil layers, which could therefore all have been formed within a few months of each other.

As we have seen, the assumption that the approximate ages of adjacent rocks can be determined radiometrically assumes that they were formed naturally rather than supernaturally, which is again an unprovable assumption. In fact scientific laws demonstrate that the earth could not have evolved naturally. In my earlier book I explained why the earth could not have been formed out of ever-expanding gases in accordance with the known behaviour of gases, nor ended up rotating on its axis in a circuit around the sun in accordance with the known laws of motion.

The geological column is falling apart

In the second place, increasing knowledge about fossils is knocking holes in the geological column. Since it was first set up, more and more fossils have been turning up in 'wrong' places.[24,25] Former index fossils such as Camptochlamys have been found in one stratum in one country and in a different stratum from a completely different geological period in another. In just ten years between 1982 and 1992 Sepkoski identified 1026 families of fossils that had apparently begun living earlier than was first believed or had continued living later than was originally believed, and could therefore no

---

[24] *Evolution pushed further into the past.* M.J.Oard, CEN Technical Journal, 10(2), pp.171–172, 1996.
[25] *How well do palaeontologists know fossil distribution?* M.J.Oard, CEN Technical Journal, 14(1), pp.7–8, 2000.

longer be used as index fossils to date a single period of time.[26] Some former index fossils, such as the coelacanth fish, which was believed to have died out 65 million years ago with the dinosaurs, have even turned up alive and well today![27]

> *Since* Lystrosaurus *has always been used to correlate rocks into time-equivalent horizons, and to place them into the Early Triassic, the Permian find of* Lystrosaurus *should now mean that Permian and Triassic are contemporaneous! An analogous line of reasoning should lead to the position that Cretaceous and Tertiary are now contemporaneous because the Upper Cretaceous genus* Parafusus *is now known from Early Tertiary rocks.*
>
> *Of course, the uniformitarians would never follow their own reasoning to its logical conclusion… In order to paper over this fatal flaw in the geologic column, uniformitarians simply back-pedal, discard* Lystrosaurus *as well as other once-esteemed index fossils as time-stratigraphic indicators, choose other index fossils as presumed time-indicators, and*

---

[26] *A compendium of fossil marine animal families.* J.J.Sepkoski, 2nd edition, Milwaukee Public Museum Contributions to Biology and Geology No. 83, p. 7, 1992.

[27] *The Coelacanth: More Living than Fossil.* Smithsonian National Museum of Natural History. vertebrates.si.edu/fishes/coelacanth/coelacanth_wider, viewed September 2017.

> *otherwise act as if nothing has happened in terms of empirical evidence. This enables them to go right on believing in such things as the Permian, Triassic, Cretaceous, and Tertiary periods. Heads I win, tails you lose.*[28]

There have been several discoveries in recent years – notably in 2005 and 2015 – of dinosaur bones that still contained flexible tissue and blood cells.[29,30] It is generally accepted that when an animal dies, soft tissues such as blood vessels, muscle and skin decay and disappear over time, so these discoveries make it extremely unlikely that the last dinosaur disappeared from the earth a massive 65 million years ago as the geological column insists. On the other hand the drowning and fossilization of dinosaurs in a worldwide flood a mere 4300 years ago or so seems far more plausible.

The fossil record supports creation, not evolution

It must be evident to any unbiased observer that the fossil record supports a belief in the Biblical account of creation rather than the theory of evolution. For one thing, if the rocks have existed since the earliest forms of life and if they

---

[28] *The fossil record: Becoming more random all the time.* J.Woodmorappe, Creation Ministries International. creation.com/the-fossil-record, viewed September 2017.

[29] *The real Jurassic Park.* S.Doyle, Creation 30(3) pp.12–15, 2008.

[30] *Fibres and cellular structures preserved in 75-million-year-old dinosaur specimens.* S.Bertazzo and others, Nature Communications 6, Article no. 7352, 2015.

contain a record of the evolution of life from its beginning until recent times then there should be a complete record of life forms from simple to complex, including multitudes of intermediate forms linking consecutive evolutionary stages. Such a record simply doesn't exist. Darwin himself acknowledged this when he wrote, '*Why, if species have descended from other species by insensibly fine gradations, do we not everywhere see innumerable transitional forms? Why is not all nature in confusion instead of species being, as we see them, well defined?*'[31]

Darwin could only surmise that the fossil record in his day must have been 'incomparably less perfect than is generally supposed'. But that argument can hardly be sustained today. Since Darwin's day not millions but billions of fossils have been recovered from all over the world. A spokesman for London's Natural History Museum wrote that '*in terms of the number of individual fossils there are probably countless billions. Most large Natural History Museums will have a collection of several million.*'[32] Yet still, in spite of all these fossil finds, there is no evidence of gradual change from one species to another as Darwin's hypothesis predicted.[33] A proper scientific theory must be supported by evidence, not mere conjecture!

It is true that from time to time there is found a fossil of something new that combines some features of two other

---

[31] *On the Origin of Species*, 1st edition. C.Darwin, John Murray, London, 1859, chapter 6, p.171.

[32] Graeme Lloyd, 4th May 2008. http://www.askabiologist.org.uk/answers/viewtopic.php?id=1408, viewed October 2016.

[33] I think that nowadays Darwin might have written 'genus' rather than 'species'.

known life forms. It is often immediately hailed in the media as 'a missing link', or sometimes even '*the* missing link' as though only two transitional stages were needed to change from one form to the other. But the only thing that a new kind of fossil proves is that something once lived that is not known to live today. It doesn't prove that one of the things it resembles evolved into the other one, or even in which direction the supposed evolution went. That is well illustrated by the fossil of a deinonychus discovered in 1969, which was identified as a bird-like dinosaur and a possible ancestor of birds, until the discovery in China of flying ancestors changed it into a bird that had lost the ability to fly.[34] So instead of being a dinosaur that was learning to fly it became a bird that had forgotten how to do it!

For another thing, although popular science gives the impression that fossils consist mainly of creatures like boring little ammonites or animals and plants that are now extinct, the vast majority are of the very same life forms as those that exist today. Stromatolites, the 'oldest' fossils on earth and supposedly 3.5 billion years old, are still being formed in lagoons in Australasia and are virtually identical.[35] Tassel ferns, Wollemi pines, fig trees, sponges, seaweed, mussels, jellyfish, starfish, horseshoe crabs (supposedly 445 million years old[36]), the amazing nautilus, coelacanths, herrings, mackerel, lobsters, crayfish, sharks, scorpions, silverfish,

---

[34] The change of status of the deinonychus is described on a plaque displaying the fossil at an exhibition at the Royal Ontario Museum in 2005. (*Feathered Dinosaurs*, The Dinosaur Museum, Blanding, UT, USA.)

[35] *Evolution's Achilles' Heels.* Ed. R.Carter, Creation Book Publishers, 2014, p. 139.

[36] Science Daily, 8 February, 2008.

spiders, cockroaches, dragonflies, frogs, tortoises, musk oxen, antelopes, reindeer, tigers, Arctic foxes, bears and horses are all fossilized examples of creatures that are alive and well today.[37,38,39]

> *Deposits found in Lincoln County, Wyoming, furnish some of the most perfect specimens of fossil fish and plants in the world… Other than fish, palm leaves from 6 to 8 feet in length and from 3 to 4 feet wide have been uncovered… an alligator was found. Several garpike, ranging in size from 4 to 6 feet have been disentombed, as have birds of about the size of the domestic chicken and resembling the snipe or plover in general conformation. In addition, specimens of sunfish, rasp-tongues, deep sea bass, chubs, pickerel and herring have been found, not to mention mollusca, crustaceans, birds, turtles, mammals and many varieties of insects.[40]*

Generally the only difference between a fossil and its living equivalent today is that sometimes the fossilized

---

[37] *Evolution's Achilles' Heels.* Ed. R.Carter, Creation Book Publishers, 2014, chapter 4.

[38] *The World of Living Fossils.* Creation Research Australia, 2003. (A DVD that shows photos of fossils and their living counterparts side by side.)

[39] *The Quaternary Era, Volume II.* Edward Arnold Co., London, 1957, p.650.

[40] *Fishing for Fossils.* Compressed Air Magazine, March 1958, volume 63, p.24.

ancestor was much larger. The true scientific evidence of the fossil record is that species have remained unchanged ever since their earliest forms.

Thus the evidence of the fossil record is that species are not evolving. Why should they? If a horseshoe crab has really remained perfectly adapted to its environment for 445 million years without succumbing to any newly evolved predators, why would it ever want to change into something else? The evidence of the fossil record is entirely consistent with the repeated refrain in Genesis chapter 1, that God created vegetation, fruit trees, sea creatures, winged birds, beasts, cattle and insects, each *'according to their kinds'*. Apart from variations within each kind (contrast an Irish wolfhound with a chihuahua) the fossil *evidence* is that flora and fauna have remained unchanged according to their kinds ever since.

So why believe in evolution?

In my earlier book I argued on logical grounds that the theory of evolution can't be true. Here I have shown that it's not supported by scientific evidence either. So why are so many scientists convinced that it *is* true? Some ardent advocates of evolution are chiefly motivated by a hatred of God or even the idea of God. But for many of them it's simply because they cannot believe in the idea of supernatural creation, and evolution is the only other way they can explain the existence of life as we know it. Some of them have openly admitted this. David Watson, who until 1951 was Professor of Zoology and Comparative Anatomy at University College, London, wrote that the theory of evolution is *'a theory universally accepted not because it can be proved by logically coherent evidence to be true but because the only alternative, special creation, is clearly incredible.'*[41]

---

[41] *Adaptation.* D.M.S.Watson, Nature, Vol. 124, 10 August 1929, p.233. The quotation and reference are given in the Wikipedia entry on D.M.S.Watson.

6

The Age Of Trees

Trees older than the earth?

The oldest living trees are believed to be around 5000 years old. This means that according to the Bible these bristlecone pine trees must have lived through the Flood, which seems most unlikely. What is not so well known is that the remains of some dead oak trees found in Germany and Switzerland are believed to be more than 13,000 years old. If that is true then according to the Bible they must have been growing before the creation of the world! Once again we have a conflict between the Bible and scientists, this time with scientists who specialize in dendrochronology.

Dendrochronology

The main method used to determine the age of a tree is to count the number of growth rings in the trunk. Each year the bark of a tree creates a ring of new wood around its trunk, and since the wood grown in springtime is lighter in colour than the slower-grown autumn wood the annual rings can be identified and counted. You've probably seen them in the stump of a tree that has been felled. So in general the number of rings is equal to the number of years that the tree has lived. Tree surgeons can discover the number of rings in a living tree by twisting a hollow auger called an increment borer into its trunk and extracting a 4mm or 5mm diameter rod of timber called a core sample. The sample displays a cross section of the growth rings without killing the tree.

Counting the growth rings does sound like a simple and foolproof method to find out how old a tree is, or how old it was when it died. So is it really possible that the tree scientists who dated the pine and oak trees could have been totally mistaken?

Bristlecone pine rings

Let's begin with the bristlecone pine trees. These apparently long-lived trees grow in the higher mountains of the south-western USA. According to researchers Ed Schulman and Tom Harlan a tree named 'Methuselah' living in the White Mountains of Colorado was 4845 years old in 2012 and another unnamed tree was 5062 years old.[42] The Wikipedia entry on 'Pinus longaeva' says that that age of the Methuselah tree was measured on an annual ring count using an increment borer. However, determining Methuselah's age was not nearly as simple as that. Schulman and Harlan themselves say, '*Ring-counted ages are derived by simple ring counts and may contain errors in age due to missing or false rings, suppressed areas, or other tree-ring anomalies*'. Therefore in the case of these very old trees the pattern of rings was

---

[42] *Rocky Mountain Tree Ring Research.* http://www.rmtrr.org/oldlist. htm, updated January 2016 and viewed October 2016.

compared with the patterns from similar adjacent trees in order to build up a more certain picture, at least back to the early years of the adjacent younger trees.

Counting the rings of the older bristlecone pine trees is particularly difficult because the bark (which is what produces the rings) doesn't extend all around the trunk. It twists in a spiral up the tree, and in the oldest specimens only a narrow strip of living tissue connects the roots to a handful of live branches. A further difficulty is that with an estimated 5000 rings each ring is only on average 0.36mm wide, making reliable identification and cross-matching even harder. Some are so thin that a microscope is needed to distinguish one from another.[43]

A paradox and its explanation

One further factor brings into question the whole basis of ring counting in the case of ancient bristlecone pines. Normally one would expect a tree planted in good soil with plenty of rain and warmth to be healthier and to live longer than a less favoured tree of the same species. In fact the apparently oldest bristlecone pine trees grow in the worst imaginable conditions, high up on cold, dry and windy mountain slopes. In the White Mountains the annual precipitation of only 250mm falls mostly as snow, and in the summer the air is said to be the driest on earth. Worse still, there is so little soil that some trees grow out of little more than a crack in the rocks. As a result what rain there is soon evaporates or drains away. Yet these particular bristlecone pines have so

---

[43] *Longevity under adversity in conifers.* E.Schulman, Science 119:398, 1954.

many rings that they appear to live about ten times longer than bristlecone pines which grow in comparatively good conditions![44] Even on the White Mountains themselves the trees on north-facing slopes appear to live twice as long as those on south-facing slopes.[45] Why should this be?

The explanation is given in a *Tree-Ring Bulletin* published way back in 1938.[46] This is a study of 'false annual rings' in Monterey pine, another species of pine and nowadays known as radiata pine. Schulman wrote: '*A double ring or multiple ring is due to the interruption of the normal course of growth of a season… such a ring is known as a false annual ring… False rings, climatic in origin, are those most commonly met with… Not infrequently climatic vicissitudes will cause not one but several false rings of this type to occur.*' In his 600-page book *The Genus Pinus*, Mirov states, '*Apparently a semblance of annual rings is formed after every rather infrequent cloudburst.*'[47]

It therefore seems certain that the bristlecone pines which grow in extremely arid conditions have developed a method of surviving by growing a little each time some moisture becomes available and then stopping until some more comes along. To my mind this is confirmed by the fact that in the central area of a stand of bristlecone pine trees,

---

[44] *Evidence for multiple ring growth per year in Bristlecone Pines.* M.Matthews, www.creation.com/bristlecone-pines, viewed October 2016.

[45] *Ancient Trees: Trees that Live for a Thousand Years.* A.Lewington & E.Parker, Collins & Brown Ltd, 1999, p.37. (This book was updated and republished by Anna Lewington in 2012.)

[46] *Classification of False Annual Rings in Monterey Pine.* E.Schulman, Tree-Ring Society, Tree-Ring Bulletin 4(3):4-7, 1938.

[47] *The Genus Pinus.* N.T.Mirov, Ronald Press Co., New York, 1967.

where growing conditions are the best, the trees do not have more than several hundred rings, whereas at the margins of the stand,[48] where the soil thins and growing conditions become progressively poorer, trees with many more rings are found.[49] It is most unlikely that such stands began with a ring of trees on poorer soil that filled in towards the middle where the soil is better over a period of perhaps a thousand years. It is surely more likely that all the trees in a stand are about the same age, and that the ones growing at the margins have more growth rings simply because they are starved for water and grow rings each time some water becomes available.

Schulman says that it is normally possible to distinguish such false rings from true annual ones, but in some cases where there is a double ring (growth in the spring and the autumn only) the two rings appear identical. Glock and colleagues demonstrated that in dry climates the band of darker wood that separates a false ring from the next one can have outer boundaries that are every bit as distinct as the outer boundaries of a true annual ring.[50] Therefore 'false rings' can be indistinguishable from 'true' annual rings. The difficulty is multiplied in the case of the bristlecone pines that have several thousand rings, for as well as being incomplete these rings are necessarily extremely thin. Since the ring pattern in similar trees in similar climatic conditions

---

[48] A stand of trees is a group of trees sufficiently uniform in every aspect to distinguish it from adjacent groups.

[49] *Environment in Relation to Age of Bristlecone Pines.* V.C.LaMarche, Ecology 50(1), 1969, pp.56-57.

[50] *Classification and multiplicity of growth layers in the branches of trees.* W.S.Glock and others, Smithsonian Miscellaneous Collections 140:1, 1960.

is likely to be similar, attempting to identify false rings by cross-matching the patterns can hardly be relied upon to identify false rings. '*The fact that the thin, entire growth layers or lenses match from one tree to another does not prove their annual character,*' Glock concluded.[51]

It is clear that bristlecone pine trees in the harshest environmental conditions grow multiple rings each year which cannot always be distinguished from annual rings. The result is that the ages of these trees cannot be determined by ring counting even with cross-matching, and attempting to do so produces apparent ages far greater than their true ages.[52] They are not 5000 years old!

Even more ancient oaks?

The oak trees that were supposed to have been alive 13,000 years ago in parts of Germany and Switzerland are a different case. Instead of talking about the longevity of living trees we are talking about pieces of dead trees and deciding when the trees that they came from were alive. The purpose of such research is to build up a database of dated growth rings so that measurements of their carbon content can be used to determine the C_{14} level in the atmosphere each year as far back as possible. An accurate knowledge of the historical

---

[51] *Classification and multiplicity of growth layers in the branches of trees.* W.S.Glock and others, Smithsonian Miscellaneous Collections 140:1, 1960, p. 275.

[52] For a critique of evidence in support of 5000 year ages see *Evidence for multiple ring growth per year in Bristlecone Pines* by M.Matthews, http://creation.com/evidence-for-multiple-ring-growth-per-year-in-bristlecone-pines, viewed October 2016.

levels of C_{14} is necessary to support the accuracy of C_{14} dating.[53,54]

None of the original trees is likely to have lived for more than 1000 years, so the method involves chaining together pieces of dead trees of successively older origin by attempting to match overlapping sections of their growth rings. The width of a growth ring depends to a large extent on the weather that year. In very dry years the tree will not grow so much and the growth ring will be narrower. So over the years there will be a pattern of thin, medium or wide growth rings that is similar in each tree, and the pattern of the first few years of a younger tree will be similar to the pattern of the last few years of an older tree that preceded it if their years of growth overlap. Provided that a continuous chain of overlapping dates can be found it is possible to continue going back in time so long as pieces of dead wood of ages that overlap still survive and can be found. Figure 2 illustrates how pieces of wood from three different trees might be chained together like this.

---

[53] *Atmospheric 14C variations derived from tree rings during the early Younger Dryas.* Q.Hua and others, Quaternary Science Reviews 28(25–26):2982–90, 2009.

[54] *Lateglacial environmental variability from Swiss tree rings.* M.Schaub and others, Quaternary Science Reviews 27(1–2): pp.29–41, 2008.

Figure 2: Growth ring chaining

The procedure seems straightforward, but it involves some serious difficulties. The first is that sequences of growth rings are not unique, especially over several thousand years, and two similar sequences might occur several centuries apart. Even in the same period the patterns of growth rings are not identical on every tree. So some judgement is required as to whether or not a pattern from one tree matches one from another, and whether it is the only possible position over a period of several thousand years that will produce such a match. By way of illustrating this, see if you can decide which of the four possible alignments of the large fragment from one tree and the small fragment from another tree is correct in Figure 3. Remember that even patterns from the same years might not match each other exactly.

Figure 3: Growth ring matching (1)

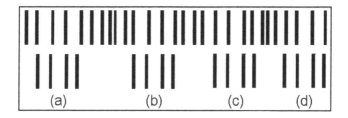

In fact none of them is right! In Figure 4 both specimens are from the same two trees as in Figure 3 except that a longer specimen from the first tree now has another 9 annual growth rings on its right-hand end. This allows an almost perfect match to be found with the specimen from the second tree.

In practice a specimen with only four annual rings would not be used to create a link in the chain: the short specimen in the diagrams is for explanatory purposes only.

Figure 4: Growth ring matching (2)

(e)

One demonstration of the uncertainties inherent in this procedure is that a chronology from Somerset in South West England and another early but detailed one from southern Germany were both 'remeasured' when a contradictory one was published by Queen's University in Belfast, Northern Ireland, even though the authors of at least the German study had previously been confident of its accuracy.[55]

Ring sequencing and C14 dating

Beyond the uncertainties regarding matching there is a still more serious problem with such databases when they go

---

[55] *A Test of Time.* D.Rohl, Arrow Books, London, Appendix C, 1996.

too far back in time. In order to make use of a piece of wood its approximate age is first determined using carbon 14 dating. An attempt is then made to match the pattern of growth rings in it with a pattern in the chain of specimens of a similar age that has already been established. If more than one good match is found, the one that is chosen will usually be the one from a date that best coincides with the C_{14} date of the new specimen. But while C_{14} dating may be fine for dates back to the pharaohs in 2625 BC it becomes wildly unreliable in the years immediately after the flood around 2300 BC, as I have explained. It inevitably indicates dates far earlier than it should because the first trees to grow after the Flood would have grown up in an atmosphere that initially had very little radioactive carbon in it. So instead of chaining together older and older pieces of tree, dendrochronologists are simply chaining together pieces of tree that happen to have less and less minute quantities of C_{14} in them. After all, it is hard to believe that specimens of wood could survive for 13,000 years without rotting away or being eaten by something, whereas they might survive in suitable conditions if they were from trees that had started to grow soon after 2300 BC and died 500 years later.

Of course, once a database of tree rings supposedly going back 13,000 years or more has been established, the tree rings can be used to 'prove' the reliability of radiocarbon dating, because C_{14} measurement of the oldest specimens in the chain will indeed indicate ages of 13,000 years or more! It's not only tree rings that are circular: the argument proving their old age is circular too!

7

Egyptian Chronology And The Date Of The Flood

The problem

The generally accepted date for the first Egyptian dynasty is earlier than the date of the Flood according to Biblical chronology.

In *Z: The Final Generation* I concluded that according to Biblical chronology the world was created in the year 3967 BC. I explained how the genealogies in Genesis enable us to calculate that the Exodus took place 2679 years after creation. In the same way it can be calculated that the Flood occurred 1656 years after creation. So if creation took place in 3967 BC the Flood would have occurred in 2311 BC. That means that the following year there would have been only eight people alive on the earth, Noah, his wife, their three sons and their wives. Yet according to Egyptologists Dodson and Hilton[56] the First Dynasty of Egypt is conjectured to have begun in 3150 BC, 839 years *before* the Flood!

---

[56] *The Complete Royal Families of Ancient Egypt.* A.Dodson & D.Hilton, Thames and Hudson, 2010.

Dating the dynasties

Although the names of some 300 Egyptian kings are known, dating them is notoriously difficult. Some surviving king lists cover many rulers but have significant gaps in their text, others provide a complete list of rulers for only a short period of Egyptian history. Some Egyptian dynasties may have overlapped, with different kings ruling in different regions at the same time rather than serially. Since the next conjectural date after the establishment of the first dynasty in 3150 is that of the final ruler of the second dynasty (the unfortunately named Nebwyhetepimyef, 2611-2584 BC), I am of the opinion that the earlier date of 3150 BC is somewhat speculative. 2611 BC however would be exactly 300 years after the Flood.

While Dodson and Hilton's book sets out the consensus of most scholars, there are a number of alternative chronologies. The 'New Chronology' was developed by the English Egyptologist David Rohl and other researchers in the 1990s. It sets the later New Kingdom dates as much as 350 years later.[57] Rohl asserts that the New Chronology allows him to identify some of the characters in the Hebrew Bible with people whose names appear in archaeological finds.

Another chronology was published privately in 1971 by Donovan Courville in his 700-page two-volume book *The Exodus Problem and Its Ramifications: A Critical Examination of the Chronological Relationships Between Israel and the Contemporary Peoples of Antiquity.*[58] He concluded that

---

[57] *A Test of Time.* D.Rohl, Cornerstone, 2001.
[58] See the Wikipedia article on 'Donovan Courville'.

Egypt was founded around 2300 BC, which would have been shortly after the Flood.

In summary, it is difficult but not impossible to reconcile the early history of Egypt with the chronology of the Bible.

8

Was Jesus Mistaken?

Introduction

There are two matters in which it appears that Jesus was mistaken. Firstly he seemed to say that he would be buried for three days, whereas he was buried for only one and a half days. More seriously he definitely seemed to teach that he would return during the lifetime of most of his hearers, but he didn't.

Jesus's burial

> *Then some of the scribes and Pharisees said to him, "Teacher, we wish to see a sign from you." But he answered them, "An evil and adulterous generation seeks for a sign; but no sign shall be given to it except the sign of the prophet Jonah. For as Jonah was three days and three nights in the belly of the whale* [sea monster], *so will the Son of man be three days and three nights in the heart of the earth."* (Matthew 12.38-40)

The Jews then said to him, "What sign have you to show us for doing this (driving traders out of the temple)*?" Jesus answered them, "Destroy this temple, and in three days I will raise it up." The Jews then said, "It has taken forty-six years to build this temple, and will you raise it up in three days?" But he spoke of the temple of his body.* (John 2.18-21)

And those who passed by derided him, wagging their heads, and saying, "Aha! You who would destroy the temple and built it in three days, save yourself, and come down from the cross!" (Mark 15.29,30)

...he was teaching his disciples, saying to them, "The Son of man will be delivered into the hands of men, and they will kill him; and when he is killed, after three days he will rise." (Mark 9.31)

"The Son of man must suffer many things, and be rejected by the elders and chief priests and scribes, and be killed, and on the third day be raised." (Luke 9.22)

That very day (the day of Jesus's resurrection) *two of them were going to a village named Emmaus... And they said to him "...our chief priests and rulers delivered him up to be condemned to death, and crucified him. But we had hoped that he was the one to*

> *redeem Israel. Yes, and besides all this, it is
> now the third day since this happened."* (Luke
> 24.13,19-21)

The Gospel writers evidently saw no contradiction in these various phrases. So far as they were concerned, 'in three days', 'after three days' and 'on the third day' all meant the same thing. The only real difficulty concerns the first quotation of Jesus, in which he said he would be three days and three nights in the heart of the earth. Even allowing for strange Jewish days that begin the previous evening, Jesus was only two nights in the 'heart of the earth', and less than two full days there.

Some Christians have solved this problem by postulating that Jesus was crucified on Thursday rather than Friday. The historical background to his last week is very complicated, but I am satisfied that Kenneth Doig has investigated every possibility in his book *New Testament Chronology*, and that his conclusion is correct, namely that Jesus was crucified on Friday in accordance with historical tradition.[59]

The explanation for Jesus's prediction that he would be buried for three days is grounded in the language of the Bible. People in Bible times counted days differently from the way we do. If the Romans wanted to say March 13th then since March 15th was known as the Ides, they called March 13th (in Latin!) three days before the Ides of March, not two days before the Ides as we would. In the Old Testament book of Esther we find Queen Esther exhorting her uncle, Mordecai, to persuade the Jews to fast in preparation for her highly risky attempt to speak to the king uninvited. "…

---

[59] *New Testament Chronology*. K.F.Doig, Edwin Mellen Press, 1990.

neither eat nor drink for three days, night or day," she said. *"I and my maids will also fast as you do."* (Esther 4.16) Yet just two verses later we read: '*On the third day Esther put on her royal robes and stood in the inner court of the king's palace…*' If three days and nights were counted in the same way as we count them today, then Esther could not have seen the king until the fourth day. Three days of day and night fasting in Bible language meant only two days in ours, just as three days and nights in the heart of the earth in Bible language meant only two days in ours.

There are other examples. For instance in Genesis 42.17-19 it says that Joseph '*…put them all together in prison for three days. On the third day Joseph said to them, "…let one of your brothers remain confined in your prison, and let the rest go…"*' Once again three days in prison in Bible language was actually only two days in ours. 1 Kings 20.29 and especially 2 Chronicles 10.5 & 12 have similar instances.

In fact the first-century rabbi Eleazar ben Azariah wrote, '*A day and night are an Onah* (a portion of time) *and the portion of an Onah is as the whole of it.*' (JT, Shabbath 9:3; BT, Pesahim 4a) This means that Jews in the time of Jesus counted any portion of a day as a whole day. So Friday evening, Saturday, and the early hours of Sunday morning counted as three days in the grave.

Jesus did not make a mistake in predicting the duration of his death, he merely counted days differently from the way we do.

The first disciples expected Jesus to return in their lifetime

The fact that Jesus did not return within the lifetime of his followers is harder to explain. For a start, there is no question that the first followers of Jesus believed he would return within their lifetime, or at least within the lifetime of most of them.

Paul wrote, '*We shall <u>not</u> all sleep* (die)*, but we <u>shall</u> all be changed, in a moment, in the twinkling of an eye, at the last trumpet. For the trumpet will sound, and the dead will be raised imperishable, and we* (i.e. those of us who are still alive and kicking) *shall be changed.*' (1 Corinthians 15.51,52)

Paul even appeared to attribute this teaching to Jesus. '*For this we declare to you by the word of the Lord, that we who are alive, who are left until the coming of the Lord, shall not precede those who have fallen asleep. For the Lord himself will descend from heaven with a cry of command, with the archangel's call, and with the sound of the trumpet of God. And the dead in Christ will rise first; then we who are alive, who are left, shall be caught up together with them in the clouds to meet the Lord in the air; and so we shall always be with the Lord.*' (1 Thessalonians 4.15-17)

Paul also said that he had received from the Lord his teaching about Holy Communion. He concluded it by saying, '*For as often as you eat this bread and drink the cup, you proclaim the Lord's death until he comes.*' (1 Corinthians 11.26). His readers couldn't have proclaimed the Lord's death 'until he comes' if he wasn't going to come back for another 2000 years. We tend to forget that Paul was addressing particular people in a church at Corinth. He was telling them to proclaim the Lord's death until he returned. A mother would tell her child, "Read a book until Daddy comes home," only if she expected him to come home shortly. Otherwise she would just say, "Read a book."

In a similar way Paul told Timothy in one of his last letters, '*I charge you to keep the commandment unstained and free from reproach until the appearing of our Lord Jesus Christ.*' (1 Timothy 6.14) Timothy couldn't do that if he were to die first.

With the possible exception of Jude, whose letter was very short, all the other writers of letters in the New Testament agreed with Paul that Jesus would return very shortly.

'*Let us hold fast the confession of our hope without wavering, …encouraging one another, and all the more as you see the Day drawing near.*' (Hebrews 10.23,25)

"*For yet a little while, and the coming one shall come and shall not tarry.*" (Hebrews 10.37)

'*The end of all things is at hand…*' (1 Peter 4.7)

'*Be patient, therefore, brethren, until the coming of the Lord.*' (James 5.7 'Until the coming of the Lord', not 'until you go to be with the Lord'.)

'*And now, little children, abide in him, so that when he appears we may have confidence and not shrink from him in shame at his coming.*' (1 John 2.28 'At his coming', not 'on the day of judgement'.)

"*Surely I am coming soon.*" (Revelation 22.20)

So either Paul, Peter, John, James and the authors of Hebrews and Revelation all misunderstood what Jesus had said about the time of his return, or else Jesus did indeed teach them that he would return within their lifetime.

This is certainly what the writers of the first three Gospels understood Jesus to have taught, as we shall now see.

The teaching of Jesus

First of all we must understand what Jesus meant by 'the Son of man'. When Jesus used this expression he had almost certainly borrowed it from a passage in the book of the prophet of Daniel. In a dream Daniel saw four beasts that clearly represented the forthcoming kingdoms of Babylon, Persia, Greece and Rome, in order. And then he wrote, *'I saw in the night visions, and behold, with the clouds of heaven there came one like a son of man, and he came to the Ancient of Days and was presented before him. And to him was given dominion and glory and kingdom, that all peoples, nations, and languages should serve him; his dominion is an everlasting dominion, which shall not pass away, and his kingdom one that shall not be destroyed.'* (Daniel 7.13,14). So whenever Jesus spoke about himself as the Son of man he was almost certainly thinking about this passage that predicted his coming on the clouds of heaven to rule the nations of the world for ever. With that in mind, it is clear that Jesus taught that he would return in the lifetime of most of his hearers. This is the unanimous record of all four writers of the Gospels.

> *These twelve* [apostles] *Jesus sent out, charging them, "Go nowhere among the Gentiles, and enter no town of the Samaritans, but go rather to the lost sheep of the house of Israel. And preach as you go, saying, 'The kingdom of heaven is at hand.' …truly, I say to you, you will not have gone through all the towns*

of Israel, before the Son of man comes." (Matthew 10.5-7,23)

"...the Son of man is to come with his angels in the glory of his Father, and then he will repay every man for what he has done. Truly, I say to you, there are some standing here who will not taste death before they see the Son of man coming in his kingdom." (Matthew 16.27,28)

"Immediately after the tribulation of those days (the fall of Jerusalem) *...they will see the Son of man coming on the clouds of heaven with power and great glory... this generation will not pass away till all these things take place."* (Matthew 24.29,30,34)

"...whoever is ashamed of me and of my words in this adulterous and sinful generation, of him will the Son of man also be ashamed, when he comes in the glory of his Father with the holy angels." And he said to them, "Truly, I say to you, there are some standing here who will not taste death before they see that the kingdom of God has come with power." (Mark 8.38-9.1)

"Truly, I say to you, this generation will not pass away before all these things take place." (Mark 13.30)

"And there will be signs in sun and moon and stars, and upon the earth distress of nations in perplexity at the roaring of the sea and the waves, men fainting with fear and with foreboding of what is coming on the world; for the powers of the heavens will be shaken. And then they will see the Son of man coming in a cloud with power and great glory. Now when these things begin to take place, look up and raise your heads, because your redemption is drawing near. … Truly I say to you, this generation will not pass away till all has taken place." (Luke 21.25-32)

When Jesus said, *"Now when these things begin to take place, look up and raise your heads, because your redemption is drawing near,"* he was speaking to his disciples. Once we take that in we discover several other passages in which he clearly told his disciples that this age would come to a close and that he would come back during their lifetime:

Now the eleven disciples went to Galilee… And Jesus came and said to them… "Go therefore and make disciples of all nations… and lo, I am with you always, to the close of the age." (Matthew 28.16-20)

"Let not your hearts be troubled; believe in God, believe also in me. In my Father's house are many rooms; if it were not so, would I have told you that I go to prepare a place for you? And when I go and prepare a place for

> *you, I will come again and will take you to*
> *myself, that where I am you may be also."*
> (John 14.1-3)

"I am the resurrection and the life," Jesus told his friend Martha after her brother Lazarus had died, *"he who believes in me, though he die, yet shall he live, and whoever lives and believes in me shall never die."* (John 11.25,26) In the first part of that sentence Jesus was talking about physical death, so we should assume that he was talking about physical death in the second part of the sentence too. Martha would certainly have understood him to mean that. So Jesus was telling her, "Anyone who has already died believing in me like Lazarus did will be raised to life again, but anyone who is still alive now and believes in me will not have to die physically but will be taken straight up to heaven in a new resurrection body." This is exactly what Paul taught when he told his readers that they would not all die but they would all be changed.

When Jesus told Martha, *"...whoever lives and believes in me shall never die,"* he must have meant that Resurrection Day and hence his return would not be far off. Perhaps that's why Paul said he had received his teaching on the subject from the Lord.

Attempted explanations

Bible commentators are understandably reluctant to accept that Jesus made a mistake, so they come up with various explanations.

- The Jewish scholar David Stern says that the word 'generation' can mean 'people' or 'race', and that when Jesus said, "This generation will not pass away before all these things take place," he was merely promising that the Jewish people as a race would survive until the end of the age. If that is what he meant then he was merely echoing God's promise in Jeremiah 31.35,36 that Israel would continue as a nation for ever. Be that as it may, it is not the natural reading of Christ's words, and it doesn't explain some of the other passages in which he said he would return in power during the lifetime of his hearers such as Mark 8.38-9.1 quoted above.

- William Barclay and other Bible commentators say that Jesus was referring only to his prophecies of the forthcoming destruction of Jerusalem when he said that his hearers would live to see it happen. In that respect Jesus was exactly right. Jerusalem fell in AD 70, 37 years after his prophecy and just within one generation of 40 years. (See Psalm 95.10) However in every passage above about Jerusalem's coming destruction Jesus also spoke about his own coming on the clouds of heaven in power and glory. And each time he said, *"Truly, I say to you, this generation will not pass away till all these things take place."* (E.g. Matthew 24.34)

- Others suggest that when Jesus said in Mark 9.1, *"...there are some standing here who will not taste death before they see that the kingdom of God has come with power,"* he meant that some of his hearers would live to see powerful miracles performed, or perhaps the powerful growth of the church as it conquered a pagan world. But his hearers had already seen Jesus cast out demons and even raise the dead, and in the previous sentence he had not been talking about the growth of the church but about the Son of man coming in the glory of his Father. Furthermore, in Mark 13.26 the phrase 'with great power' clearly referred not to miracles nor the growth of the church but to Jesus's return. *"And then they will see the Son of man coming in clouds <u>with great power</u> and glory."*

In all these prophetic passages the coming of the kingdom of God is unambiguously equated, not with the spreading of the gospel but with the return of Jesus as king. Where Luke concludes, *"…when you see these things taking place, you know that the kingdom of God is near,"* (Luke 21.31) Matthew's version is, *"…when you see all these things, you know that he is near, at the very gates."* (Matthew 24.33) The kingdom of God is equated with Christ's return. So when Jesus said in Mark 9.1, *"…There are some standing here who will not taste death before they see that the kingdom of God has come with power,"* he was simply referring to his return in power and glory to establish the promised kingdom of God. And there is no getting away from the fact that he said that this would take place while at least some of his hearers were still alive.

Most Christian preachers and Christians solve the problem by reinterpreting the meaning of the kingdom of God to mean living with Jesus as king. Certainly when we do that then in a limited sense the kingdom of God has already come among us. But a minority of the population imperfectly obeying Jesus Christ on this present earth falls far short of the amazing promises about God's kingdom made by the Old Testament prophets. (Isaiah 65.17-25; Micah 4.1-4 and Zechariah 14.1-9) Those promises that God's kingdom of righteousness will one day be established throughout the earth have still not yet been fulfilled, in spite of the fact that Jesus said their fulfilment was imminent. In fact many Jews would regard this as evidence that Jesus was *not* the Messiah. In Jewish eyes the kingdom of God has not come even now, let alone during the lifetime of the apostles. In any case, Jesus didn't only say that his hearers would live to see the kingdom of God come: he also said they would live to see him return.

No misunderstanding

So Jesus clearly taught that he would return to inaugurate the promised kingdom of God within the lifetime of his hearers. The writers of the Gospels and Epistles did not misunderstand what he said. How could they have done? For almost six weeks after his resurrection he appeared to most of them, '*speaking of the kingdom of God*'. (Acts 1.3) As a result they unanimously understood that he would come back from heaven to establish the kingdom before they all died.

In fact Jesus's very first words in Mark's Gospel carried this selfsame message. '*…Jesus came into Galilee, preaching the gospel of God, and saying, "The time is fulfilled, and the kingdom of God is at hand; repent, and believe in the gospel."*' (Mark 1.14,15) The good news that Jesus announced was not that God was going to establish his promised kingdom. That wouldn't even have been news at all, for his Jewish audience knew he was going to do that one day. The good news that Jesus proclaimed was not that God was going to inaugurate his promised kingdom, but that he was going to do it imminently, that its inauguration was at hand. *That* was the good news he brought. The promised new age, when men would beat their swords into ploughshares and the wolf would lie down with the lamb and unrighteousness and injustice would cease for ever under the everlasting worldwide reign of the promised Messiah was just round the corner! They were the generation that was going to see it happen! That was the good news Jesus told them to believe. Why would he have said it was good news if God's kingdom wasn't going to come for another 2000 years? If they were going to have to wait another 2000 years it would have been bad news, not good news!

Contrary teaching

It's true that some passages in the Gospels suggest that the kingdom will be a long time in coming. Luke tells us that Jesus '...*proceeded to tell a parable, because he was near to Jerusalem, and because they supposed that the kingdom of God was to appear immediately.*' (Luke 19.11) This parable was about a nobleman who went away to receive a kingdom and then return. Nevertheless it does not say that the nobleman was away for a long time. Through the parable Jesus was simply telling people that when he rode into Jerusalem on a donkey the following week he would not be announcing an immediate Jewish Brexit from the Roman Empire, with himself as the de facto king. He was telling them that he had to leave the earth first and then return as king. In the parable the nobleman returned to the very same servants that he had left behind, so if it tells us anything about Jesus's intentions then once again it is telling us that he expected to return to the earth in the lifetime of the same people who saw him leave it.

In Matthew's Gospel Jesus told two other parables about his return – the parable of the wise and foolish maidens awaiting the coming of the bridegroom, and the one about a master who gave his three stewards some talents of silver to invest on his behalf while he was away. In the first parable the bridegroom's return is delayed, and in the second one the master is away for a long time. (Matthew 25.1-30) However a delayed return and a long time away are only relative to expectations. In the first story the bridegroom did eventually return that same night, and in the second one he returned to the same stewards he had left, as in the story of the nobleman. The main point of both stories was not that Jesus would be away for a long time, but that we must be ready for him when he comes back.

More importantly perhaps are the three main passages of prophecy recorded by Matthew, Mark and Luke. They are all similar, and in each one Jesus said that many things had to happen before he returned. *'As he sat on the Mount of Olives, the disciples came to him privately, saying, "Tell us… what will be the sign of your coming and of the close of the age?"'* (Matthew 24.3) He replied, *"…you will hear of wars and rumours of wars… but the end is not yet. …there will be famines and earthquakes in various places: all this is but the beginning of the birth-pangs."* (Matthew 24.6-8). Jesus then told his disciples they would be hated and put to death; many believers would fall away and betray other believers; false prophets would arise; and only when the gospel of the kingdom had been preached throughout the whole world would the end come. (Matthew 24.9-14) How could Jesus say that all those things had to take place and that the gospel would be preached throughout the world before he returned if he was going to return during the lifetime of his hearers?

There are three possible explanations of all this.

A mistake?

The most obvious, but somewhat unwelcome, explanation is that Jesus simply made a mistake. After saying, *"...this generation will not pass away before all these things take place,"* he added, *"But of that day or that hour no one knows, not even the angels in heaven, nor the Son, but only the Father."* (Mark 13.30,32). But if as he said he didn't know when he would return, why was he so confident it would be within the lifetime of his hearers?

When Jesus was made a man he left behind everything that belonged to divinity and became just like us, except that he was without sin. (Philippians 2.6,7; Hebrews 4.15) As God Jesus could know everything, but as a man it was no longer possible. He could no longer know the position of every atom in the universe for there were not enough cells in his human brain to contain so much information. He would not have known about radioactivity or black holes or how big the earth was, and without knowing the extent of the earth he might well have considered it possible to evangelize the whole world as he knew it within a generation.

Nevertheless, since Jesus said that he taught only what the Father told him to, and that he always told the truth, it is hard to believe that Jesus's Father would have allowed him to make such an important mistake, if that is what it was.

A Jewish gospel

A more credible explanation is that God did indeed intend the world to be evangelized within a generation, but only the *Jewish* world. And then, when the Jews rejected the message, God replaced Plan A by Plan B, which was the evangelization of the Gentiles. Obviously that task would take much longer. This is the explanation given by Michael Penny and others.[60] And to a large extent the New Testament does seem to support this view.

When Jesus sent his disciples out on a training mission, he said, *"Go nowhere among the Gentiles, and enter no town of the Samaritans, but go rather to the lost sheep of the house of Israel. And preach as you go, saying, 'The kingdom of heaven is at hand.'"* (Matthew 10.5-7) In Matthew 15.24 Jesus said, *"I was sent only to the lost sheep of the house of Israel,"* and in John's Gospel his final words of commission to his disciples, after his resurrection, were, *"As the Father has sent me, even so I send you."* (John 20.21) The implication of this was that his disciples too should preach only to Jews. And when he said in Matthew 10.23, *"…you will not have gone through all the towns of Israel, before the Son of man comes,"* he was evidently talking about the spread of the gospel, not throughout the

---

[60] *A Key to Unfulfilled Prophecy.* M.Penny, The Open Bible Trust, Reading, Great Britain, 2011.

whole inhabited earth, but only in those towns where there were Israelites – settlements of Jews.

This certainly seems to have been how the early believers understood Jesus's intentions. In Acts 11.19 Luke tells us that '...*those who were scattered because of the persecution that arose over Stephen travelled as far as Phoenicia and Cyprus and Antioch, speaking the word to none except Jews.*' When Peter was eventually persuaded to preach the gospel to a Gentile, he and the believers with him were astonished when God poured out his Spirit on the Roman centurion Cornelius and his household. (Acts 10.44-48) Why would they have been so surprised if Jesus had clearly told them to preach to Gentiles as well as Jews?

So why did Jesus not return when the gospel had been preached to Jews in all the towns where they had settled? According to Penny and others it was because God's promise that Christ would return in power and glory had a condition attached to it. In Acts chapter 3 Peter reminded a crowd of Jews who had gathered outside the temple in Jerusalem that they had collaborated in crucifying their Messiah. He then concluded, *"Repent therefore, and turn again, that your sins may be blotted out... and that* [the Lord] *may send the Christ appointed for you, Jesus, whom heaven must receive until the time for establishing all that God spoke by the mouth of his holy prophets from of old."* (Acts 3.19-21) The promise of Christ's return was dependent on the Jews' repentance. And while many Jews did repent of their unbelief in Jesus, the Jews as a nation did not do so. The consequence was that their sins were not blotted out, the promised Christ did not return to them, and instead of living to see the return of the Son of

Man, they saw the destruction of their temple and much of the holy city by the Romans just 40 years later.

A change of plan

Plan A was indeed that the Jewish nation as a whole should return to God and that their promised Messiah would then return in power and glory. Nevertheless they rejected the gospel as a nation, unwilling or unable to believe that Jesus was their promised Messiah, so the Gentile world was evangelized instead. This change of plan was already becoming evident in Acts 18.5-6 when Paul was in Corinth. '*When Silas and Timothy arrived from Macedo'nia, Paul was occupied with preaching, testifying to the Jews that the Christ was Jesus. And when they opposed and reviled him, he shook out his garments and said to them, "Your blood be upon your heads! I am innocent. From now on I will go to the Gentiles."*'

In fact the book of Acts seems to conclude with an announcement of this change of plan:

> *When* [the local leaders of the Jews in Rome] *had appointed a day for* [Paul]*, they came to him at his lodging in great numbers. And he expounded* [the gospel] *to them from morning till evening, testifying to the kingdom of God and trying to convince them about Jesus both from the law of Moses and from the prophets. And some were convinced by what he said, while others disbelieved. So, as they disagreed among themselves, they departed, after Paul had made one statement: "The Holy Spirit was right in saying to your fathers through*

Isaiah the prophet: 'Go to this people, and say,
You shall indeed hear but never understand,
and you shall indeed see but never perceive…'
Let it be known to you then that this salvation
of God has been sent to the Gentiles; they will
listen." (Acts 28.23-29)

The question is, would God really have changed his plan? Would he not have known what would happen? Could he really have intended the gospel to be preached only to Jews in the known world within a generation, and then adopt a totally different plan to have the gospel preached to Gentiles throughout the whole world instead? Jeremiah 18.9 & 10 says, "Yes, he could!" *"…if at any time I declare concerning a nation or a kingdom that I will build and plant it, and if it does evil in my sight, not listening to my voice, then I will repent of the good which I had intended to do to it."*

An Old Testament example and a New Testament prediction

The most obvious example of a change of plan concerns God's promise to lead a nation of slaves out of captivity in Egypt into a new land. When Moses first encountered the Lord God at the burning bush, the Lord told him to say to the people of Israel, *"…I promise that I will bring you up out of the affliction of Egypt, to the land of the Canaanites… a land flowing with milk and honey."* (Exodus 3.17) On the day that the Israelites escaped from Egypt Moses told the people, *"…When the Lord brings you into the land of the Canaanites, as he swore to you and your fathers, and shall give it to you, you shall set apart to the Lord all that first opens the womb."* (Exodus 13.11,12) Some months later the Lord said, *"Behold, I send an angel before you, to guard you on the way and to bring you to the place which I have prepared."* (Exodus 23.20) And a little over a year later, when the Lord had welded his people into a nation with comprehensive laws and a judicial system; a priesthood, a tabernacle and religious rituals; a weekly and annual timetable for work, rest and holidays; and an army trained in warfare through a successful battle with the Amalekites; finally the time to fulfil his promise arrived. *'The Lord said to Moses, "Send men to spy out the land of Canaan, which I give to the people of Israel."'* (Numbers 13.1,2)

Again and again God promised the people who had been Pharaoh's slaves that he would bring them into the land of Canaan. Yet he did not keep that promise! He left almost all of them to die in the wilderness! Why? Did he make an honest mistake? Did he lie to them? No. It was truly his intention. But when the time came for them to enter the new land and defeat its idolatrous inhabitants in battle the people were too frightened to do it. *"The land, through which we have gone to spy it out, is a land that devours its inhabitants; and all the people that we saw in it are men of great stature. ...and we seemed to ourselves like grasshoppers, and so we seemed to them."* (Numbers 13.32,33) The result of their cowardice, unbelief and disobedience was that the generation who had been promised the land of Canaan never saw it, and it was left for the following generation to inherit the promise. *'...they were unable to enter because of their unbelief.'* (Hebrews 3.19)

Like other events and prophecies in the Old Testament, what happened in the wilderness was precisely mirrored in the New Testament. The Lord Jesus promised his own generation that they would live to see and enter the kingdom of God, but they failed to do so because they did not, as a nation, believe in him. As the years went by Paul, the ex-rabbi, began to wrestle in his mind with the terrible fact that his own beloved nation was as a whole continuing to reject her Messiah. He wondered whether this meant that God had rejected the Jews for ever. He came to the conclusion that what had happened was in fact for the benefit of Gentiles, who would otherwise not have had an equal share in God's blessings. And he believed that God would bring the Jewish nation back to faith once the full number of the Gentiles had come into the kingdom. (Romans 11.11,12,25-27)

To be honest it is not strictly true to talk about a Plan A and a Plan B. There was only one plan, but it had several stages. In Acts 2.23 Peter told the listening crowd that Jesus was '*delivered up according to the definite plan and foreknowledge of God*'. In other words, God knew beforehand that the Jewish leaders in Jerusalem would reject Jesus as their Messiah, yet he went ahead and sent his Son into the world for their salvation. In just the same way, he knew that they would continue to reject Jesus after he had ascended to heaven, yet he went ahead and told his apostles to preach Christ to the Jewish race throughout the known world, in order to give them a further opportunity to receive him as their saviour and King. It was only after they refused this opportunity too that he inaugurated the next stage of his plan, which was to have the gospel preached to Gentiles and to invite them to join his kingdom on equal terms with his chosen race.

The interesting thing is that Jesus predicted all this would happen:

> *The kingdom of heaven may be compared to a king who gave a marriage feast for his son, and sent his servants to call those who were invited to the marriage feast; but they would not come. …they made light of it and went off, one to his farm, another to his business, while the rest seized his servants, treated them shamefully, and killed them. The king was angry, and he sent his troops and destroyed those murderers and burned their city. Then he said to his servants, "The wedding is ready, but those invited were not worthy. Go therefore to the thoroughfares, and invite to the marriage feast as many as you find."*
> (Matthew 22.1-10)

Notice that the parable even included a prediction of the martyrdom of some of the early church leaders and the forthcoming destruction of the city of Jerusalem. It is hard to conclude that Jesus really didn't know exactly how things were going to work out!

A gospel for all nations

Nevertheless, there is an alternative and fascinating explanation for Jesus's failure to return in the lifetime of his hearers as he had promised.

In the first place, Jesus did indeed command his apostles to preach the gospel to all nations, and not only to the Jewish people. In Matthew 28.18,19 he gave his remaining eleven apostles this great commission: *"All authority in heaven and on earth has been given to me. Go therefore and make disciples of all nations..."* The Greek literally says, 'disciple all the nations', not 'make disciples from among all the nations'. Furthermore the Greek word *ethna*, translated here as 'nations', is often used in the New Testament to mean the Gentile nations as *distinct from* the Jewish nation! For example, in Matthew 4.15 and 6.32, where the Authorized Version and the Revised Standard Version speak of 'Gentiles', the Greek word is actually *ethna*! So Christ's commission to his disciples at the end of Matthew's Gospel was clearly to preach the gospel *to* all nations, and *especially* to the non-Jewish nations.

Jesus's intention was just as explicit in the Gospels of Luke and Mark. In Luke 24.46,47 we read, '...*and* [Jesus] *said to them, "Thus it is written, that the Christ should suffer and on the third day rise from the dead, and that repentance and forgiveness of sins should be preached in his name to all nations, beginning from Jerusalem."'* The Greek unambiguously states, 'to all the nations', not 'in all the world'. Mark's account of Christ's instructions to his disciples is even more inclusive. *'And he said to them, "Go into all the world and preach the gospel to the whole creation"'*! (Mark 16.15) How could 'the whole creation' possibly have meant only Jews?

And if that isn't enough, there are at least 58 verses in the Old Testament, from Genesis to Malachi, that say God's concern is for 'all nations', 'all peoples', 'all mankind', 'all creation', 'every creature', 'every knee', 'every tongue', 'men of every language' and 'the world' to know and worship him.[61] And Jesus said he had come to fulfil the law and the prophets. (Matthew 5.17)

It is true that Jesus said he was sent only to the lost sheep of the tribe of Israel during his first visit to the earth. In a ministry lasting little more than two years there was no time to preach to Gentiles as well as Jews. But when some Greek-speaking Gentiles wanted to meet Jesus during his final week here he said that after his death and resurrection things would be different. *"I, when I am lifted up from the earth, will draw all men to myself,"* he said. (John 12.32)

At the end of Matthew's Gospel Jesus promised his eleven remaining apostles, *"…lo, I am with you always, to the close of the age."* The implication seems clear. When the apostles had finished their task of preaching to all nations the end of the age would come. They might have thought that to preach to all nations within their lifetime was an impossible task, but the fact is that they could have done it, and they could have completed the task long before they died! They could have completed the task quite easily by the power of *multiplication.*

The power of multiplication

Back in the garden of Eden the Lord told Adam and Eve to *'be fruitful and multiply, and fill the earth…'* If they thought that to be an impossible task it was because they had not reckoned on the power of multiplication. Because they

---

[61] At the time of writing (April 2018) the verses mentioned are listed at www.ywam.org/get-involved-2/all-nations-verse-list. There are another 29 similar verses in the New Testament that speak of God's desire for people from every ethnic group to know and worship him.

were fruitful and made a good number of children (Genesis 5.3,4), and because each of their children gave birth to a good number of children too (Genesis 5.6,7), two people eventually filled the earth with people.

In the same way Jesus told his remaining eleven apostles to *"…make disciples of all nations… teaching them to observe all that I have commanded you."* (Matthew 28.19,20) They too must have thought it an impossible task to make disciples of all nations. But it wasn't impossible, because Jesus also told them to teach their disciples to do the same thing that he had commanded them to do. It's exactly what Paul told his disciple Timothy to do. '*…what you have heard from me before many witnesses entrust to faithful men who will be able to teach others also.*' (2 Timothy 2.2) Once again it's the principle of multiplication at work. If each wave of converts had taught the next wave to do the same, and if they had taught their converts in turn to do the same, then the whole world could have been reached *in one generation* through the process of multiplication. And that's what began to happen in the very beginning. When only Peter and the other apostles were preaching in Jerusalem '*…the Lord added to their number day by day those who were being saved*'. (Acts 2.47) But when the church spread throughout Judea and Galilee and Samaria and everybody began to share the good news with their neighbours the number of believers *multiplied*. (Acts 9.31)

Some six months after the day of Pentecost, Stephen was stoned to death. The new believers in Jerusalem fled to other parts of the country where they preached the word. (Acts 8.1-4) But suppose that they and every subsequent believer had been willing to keep moving on in order to continue to share the good news of Jesus where it had never been heard before. And suppose that each believer led just *one* other person to believe in Jesus each year and that every new believer did the same. That's feasible, wouldn't you say? The astonishing fact is that if that had happened then within just sixteen years the first group of 3000 Christians who were baptized on the day of Pentecost would have multiplied to almost 200 million, the estimated population of the entire world at that time! Just sixteen years!

Let's say that at Pentecost in the year AD 30 there were 3000 Christians altogether. In the year AD 31 the number would have doubled to 6000, in AD 32 it would have doubled again to 12,000, and so on. If you keep doubling the number you'll find that by AD 46 it will have reached 196.6 million! (Enter 3000x2^16 in your calculator if you don't believe me.) And that's not all. Not everyone who heard the gospel would have accepted it: perhaps only one in ten would have done so. In that case the task of converting 20 million people to Christ rather than 200 million could have been accomplished *in less than thirteen years*!

To be fair, the calculations assume that no one would have died during that period. And in order for the multiplication process to continue as calculated, many or perhaps most believers would have had to move to new places and even new countries as the evangelization of their current locations was completed. But this is exactly what Jesus expected many Christians to do. In Luke 18.29,30 he said, *"...there is no man who has left house or wife or brothers or parents or children, for the sake of the kingdom of God, who will not receive manifold more in this time, and in the age to come eternal life."* And in Luke 14.33 he said, *"...whoever of you does not renounce* (give up) *all that he has cannot by my disciple."*

In practice some Christians with family responsibilities, health problems or a lack of zeal would have stayed put or fizzled out as evangelists. Nevertheless others on fire with the Holy Spirit could easily have made up for that by leading far more than one person to Christ every year. Multitudes of Samaritans responded to Philip's preaching, for example, and he wasn't even an apostle. (Acts 8.5,6)

It seems certain to me that the task of preaching the gospel to everyone on earth could have been accomplished well within one generation if the majority of believers and their converts had obeyed Christ's instructions to multiply! One reason that he kept telling people he might return at any time was surely to instill a sense of urgency into their evangelism.

The principle of multiplication was evidently in the mind of Jesus in his parable of the yeast or leaven. *"To what shall I compare the kingdom of God? It is like leaven which a woman took and hid in three measures of flour, till it was all leavened."* (Luke 13.20,21) Yeast cells divide, reproduce and multiply. And while my calculations are based on everyone leading one person a year to Christ for a maximum of sixteen years, I believe that Jesus envisaged his followers leading significantly more than sixteen other people to faith during their lifetime. In his parable of the sower he said that the good soil represented people *"...who hear the word and accept it and bear fruit, thirtyfold and sixtyfold and a hundredfold."* (Mark 4.20) So it really isn't surprising that Jesus expected the task of world evangelization to be completed within a generation. It could have been!

I know that before the age of translation apps and transatlantic aircraft there would have been problems concerning language and travel to distant continents, but with God all things are possible. He demonstrated on the day of Pentecost that the gift of tongues could cross language barriers, and perhaps that was intended to be its chief purpose. And even if God didn't enable people to walk across the sea as he enabled Jesus to do, or to move someone supernaturally from one place to another as he appears to have done with Philip in Acts 8.40, they did have ships in those days, and the Bering Strait between Russia and Alaska in North America is only 55 miles wide at its narrowest point.

So it seems to me that, in the mind of Jesus, his disciples and their converts would spread the gospel throughout the earth by the process of multiplication within a generation, and that in consequence he would be able to return before they all died of old age. And it was not unrealistic for him to believe this, even if as a man he didn't know just how vast the earth was. He intended the first apostles to blaze a trail into every land on the earth, and the resulting believers to commit their lives fully to spreading the message of Jesus Christ and his kingdom in the power of the Holy Spirit during the few years before his return. They were to forsake everything else and take up their cross to follow him. (Luke 14.25-27,33)

Even before the Holy Spirit was given at Pentecost Jesus sent out 72 men on a training run to tell people that the kingdom of God was near and to heal the sick. (Luke 10.1-9,17) And Jesus reinforced his plan to involve *all* believers in evangelism on the day of his ascension. He told his eleven apostles, *"Go into all the world and preach the gospel to the whole creation. ...these signs will accompany those who believe: in my name they will cast out demons; they will speak in new tongues; they will pick up serpents, and if they drink any deadly thing, it will not hurt them; they will lay their hands on the sick, and they will recover."* (Mark 16.15-18) Clearly *all* the new believers were to be equipped to proclaim Christ in the power of the Holy Spirit, not merely the apostles. That was the plan that Jesus announced, and if it had been fulfilled then centuries of warfare would have been avoided and countless millions of people would not have been killed in the succeeding centuries by warfare, drought, flood, famine and plague.

So what went wrong?

When the vision fades

Although the early Christian church was in many ways amazing and changed the world, it was far from perfect. There were quarrels and disputes in it (James 4.1; Acts 15.39; Galatians 2.11); jealousy and strife (1 Corinthians 3.3); instances of serious sexual immorality (1 Corinthians 5.1); and early departures from faith in Christ (Galatians 3.1-3). It also seems that both the apostles and most of the early Christians never fully grasped the vision that they were to preach the gospel to the whole world and to dedicate their lives to that one overriding purpose. For consider these facts:

- Jesus had commanded his eleven apostles to be his witnesses 'in Jerusalem and in all Judea and Samaria and to the end of the earth' (Acts 1.8), yet they remained in Jerusalem for at least another seventeen years (Galatians 1.18 and 2.1,9).

- Peter, John and other 'pillars' of the church decided that their ministry was to be confined to Jews (Galatians 2.9) when Jesus had clearly commanded *all* the apostles to preach the gospel to *all* nations (Matthew 28.19; Mark 16.15; Luke 24.47,48; Acts 1.8).

- They decided (Galatians 2.9) that only Paul and Barnabas should preach to Gentiles, at a time when Gentiles outnumbered Jews by 50 to 1!

- Instead of 'declaring the wonderful deeds of him who called you out of darkness into his marvellous light' (1 Peter 2.9) many ordinary believers became lukewarm (Revelation 3.15,16). They abandoned their first love for Jesus (Revelation 2.4) and became spiritually dead (Revelation 3.1), just as Jesus had predicted they would (Matthew 24.12).

Of course it's easy for us to be critical: most of us haven't experienced the opposition, threats, arrests or the risk of martyrdom that many of those early Christians faced daily. Nevertheless it seems to me that although things began very well, within a few years both the original apostles and the first generation of Christians largely abandoned the worldwide mission Jesus had given to them. In consequence, even though the church still grew rapidly within the confines of the Roman Empire, that first generation of believers never lived to see Christ's return. The promise Jesus had repeatedly made that he would return within their lifetime to set up the kingdom of God was never fulfilled, just as God never fulfilled his promise to the slaves in Egypt to bring them into the land of Canaan. Nearly all God's promises, perhaps all of them, come with conditions!

What about us?

I cannot possibly finish this chapter without applying its lessons to us. If you, like me, have committed your life to Jesus Christ and his mission, what are we doing about sharing the good news of eternal life?

According to the research I described in my book, *Z: The Final Generation*, Jesus is finally going to return in or around the year 2033. Evacuation day, when believers in Christ will leave the earth prior to his return, should be in 2030. So depending on when you are reading this book, you may have only five years or so left to encourage those you know or love to put their trust in Christ. There are many ways to do this, but in my opinion there are four things we all have to do first:

- Join a church! If possible join a lively church which is committed to leading people to Christ. This will give you essential encouragement, provide you with sound teaching and resources such as *Why Jesus?* and *Why Christmas?* booklets, and give you opportunities to invite people to social or evangelistic events, such as an Alpha course. If joining a lively church in your neighbourhood isn't possible then at least ask the Lord to help you to find one or two other Christians that you can share with and pray with regularly so that you can support and encourage each other in your outreach for Christ. According to John Wesley, *'the Bible knows nothing of solitary religion'.*

- <u>Know the gospel!</u> Soon after I began my ministry two members of my congregation asked me how they could know God personally. I didn't know how to answer them! If we are unclear ourselves what the good news is and why people need to hear it, how can we hope to share it with them effectively? If no one in your church can explain it to you in a way that you can understand, find two or three other Christians and try to sort out together what you believe with the help of the Bible. If you think it would help, practise sharing this with each other. That's how sales staff are trained, and we have something far more important to offer than vacuum cleaners, sports cars or life insurance. Practise what you'll preach! No one became an expert in anything without practice.

- <u>Love your neighbours</u>! Make an effort to get to know your neighbours, colleagues, fellow students, etc. Help them practically when you can; help with homework, baby-sitting, car lifts or translation; be hospitable, visit them when they are in need, offer to pray with them when they are sick; go the extra mile. Putting love into practice softens the soil of the heart. And when the Holy Spirit gives an opportunity to share the word of God with them, it can then take root and perhaps produce the fruit of eternal life.

- <u>Pray for people to be saved</u>! We are engaged in a spiritual battle for human souls, and this requires spiritual weapons. Above all it requires Spirit-empowered prayer. A principal result of praying for unsaved members of your family, school, college, workplace or neighbourhood is that it will keep you alert and willing to share God's love in word or deed with them whenever he provides you with an opportunity to do so. Pray for yourself too, asking the Lord to make you bold in speaking and acting as Christ's representative. My wife prays that for me every day, because she knows that I need it!

Today there are believers in Christ throughout the world. There are believers in countries like Cuba, Iran, North Korea and even in our own country! If believers currently number only 1% of a nation's population, the fact remains that if each one were to introduce one person to Christ every year and teach them to do the same then a third of the population would be in God's kingdom within five years. And since Jesus said that relatively few people will find the way to life, that would surely be more than enough to prepare the world for his return!

> *Rise up, O men of God! Have done with lesser things;*
> *Give heart and soul and mind and strength to serve the King of kings.*

William Pearson Merrill

9

The Destiny Of
The Damned

Introduction

Many people find the idea of hell abhorrent. The idea that a loving, merciful God could destine unbelievers to spend eternity being tormented in unquenchable fire seems totally incomprehensible, especially if their only crime is that they've never heard of Jesus. So in this chapter I've tried to discover what the Bible really teaches regarding the final destiny of those who will not inherit eternal life.

Words

> "When I use a word," Humpty Dumpty said, in rather a scornful tone, "it means just what I choose it to mean – neither more nor less."
> "The question is," said Alice, "whether you can make words mean so many different things.'
>
> Lewis Carroll,
> *Alice's Adventures in Wonderland*

Words are like curtains: they can shut out the light or let it in. In the original Hebrew and Greek of the Bible there are several different words for where people go when they die. Gehenna has a very different meaning from Sheol and Hades, and none of them means what is popularly thought of as hell. Nevertheless the Authorized (King James) Version translates all three words as 'hell'. This is confusing and it obscures the truth. Even my favourite Revised Standard Version translates Gehenna as hell.

Let's begin by drawing the curtains apart to see what these various words meant.

(i) Sheol

The Hebrew word 'Sheol' literally means 'the unseen state'. It is used as a synonym for death. After God had delivered David from all his enemies he sang, *"the cords of Sheol entangled me, the snares of death confronted me."* (2 Samuel 22.6) Describing a 'loose woman' Proverbs 5.5 says, *'Her feet go down to death; her steps follow the path to Sheol.'*

However Sheol also seems to be regarded as a place beneath the earth. *'If I ascend to heaven, thou art there! If I make my bed in Sheol, thou art there!'* (Psalm 139.8) *"Son of man, wail over the multitude of Egypt, and send them down… to the nether world, to those who have gone down to the Pit… The mighty chiefs shall speak of them, with their helpers, out of the midst of Sheol: 'They have come down, they lie still, the uncircumcised, slain by the sword.'"* (Ezekiel 32.18,21)

In the Old Testament Sheol is everybody's destiny at death, at least until a day of judgement comes. In itself it is neither good nor bad. *'There the wicked cease from troubling, and there the weary are at rest. There the prisoners are at ease together; they hear not the voice of the taskmaster. The small and the great are there, and the slave is free from his master.'* (Job 3.17-19)

(ii) The Pit

'The Pit' is an expression often used in the Old Testament as a synonym for Sheol. *'O Lord, thou hast brought up my soul from Sheol, restored me to life from among those gone down to the Pit.'* (Psalm 30.3) To the evil city of Tyre God said, *"...I will thrust you down with those who descend into the Pit, to the people of old, and I will make you to dwell in the nether world, among primeval ruins, with those who go down to the Pit, so that you will not be inhabited or have a place in the land of the living."* (Ezekiel 26.20)

(iii) The dust

The Old Testament teaches that when we die our bodies decompose, but our spirits live on in a state akin to sleep, awaiting a day of judgement. *'...when thou takest away their breath, they die and return to their dust.'* (Psalm 104.29) *'... the dust returns to the earth as it was, and the spirit returns to God who gave it.'* (Ecclesiastes 12.7) *'...for now shall I sleep in the dust.'* (Job 7.21 AV) *'...many of those who sleep in the dust of the earth shall awake, some to everlasting life, and some to shame and everlasting contempt.'* (Daniel 12.2)

With none of these Old Testament words is there any suggestion of punishment, flames or torture following death.

(iv) Hades

In the New Testament the Greek word *hadēs* literally means 'the unseen world'. Hades is the exact equivalent of Sheol. In Psalm 16.10 David had declared, '*...thou dost not give me up to Sheol, or let thy godly one see the Pit.*' When Peter quoted the Greek version of this same Psalm in Acts 2.27 he said, '*For thou wilt not abandon my soul to Hades, nor let thy Holy One see corruption.*' Hades is Sheol.

Again it seems to be regarded as a place. "*And you, Caperna-um, will you be exalted to heaven? You shall be brought down to Hades.*" (Luke 10.15) "*...I will build my church, and the powers of death* (Greek: 'gates of Hades') *shall not prevail against it.*" (Matthew 16.18) However it is not identical to death, because Revelation 20.14 speaks of Death *and* Hades.

Hades is the place or state into which people enter at death to await the day of judgement; at least it is if they don't die as believers in Jesus Christ.

Hades will continue to exist until the day of judgement. After that, when no further people will be born and death will be abolished, Hades will be destroyed. '*And I saw the dead, great and small, standing before the throne, and books were opened. ...Death and Hades gave up the dead in them, and all were judged by what they had done. Then Death and Hades were thrown into the lake of fire.*' (Revelation 20.12-14)

(v) Gehenna

The other Greek word translated in the Authorized Version as 'hell' is *geenna*, which is normally pronounced and written as 'Gehenna'.

Gehenna was a rubbish tip outside Jerusalem, a place more accurately known as the Valley of Hinnom. It's still there, to the south-west of the old city of Jerusalem, but nowadays it's mostly covered by grass. It is not some place 'under the earth', neither is it the opposite of heaven. Whenever Jesus used the word 'Gehenna' he meant simply 'the rubbish tip'. Bible commentators generally agree that the valley was used to dispose of animal carcasses, rubbish and perhaps also the corpses of executed criminals. They were either burned up or eaten by maggots, so it was an appropriate word for a place of destruction. In the first century one corner was used as a proper burial ground, and the Jewish historian Josephus recorded that the tomb of Annas the high priest was located there.

(vi) Hell

The English word 'hell' originally meant much the same as Sheol or Hades, the netherworld of the dead. But in the Middle Ages it came to mean something far worse. The terrifying paintings of hell produced during mediaeval and Renaissance times reflected and reinforced a belief that the final destiny of the wicked is to be tormented for ever in the presence of the devil and his angels. However Michelangelo's fresco of the *Last Judgement* on the wall behind the altar in the Sistine Chapel is particularly frightening, not because it depicts horrible demons toasting human beings for supper as some earlier paintings did, but because the terrified men and women on the wrong side of Jesus at Judgement Day appear so lifelike. Of course it was in the interests of the mediaeval church to propagate such beliefs and at the same time to teach that salvation was found only in the church. It ensured faithful church attendance and full offering plates!

There is no evidence in the Bible that hell as it is popularly envisaged is a real place at all. Genesis says that in the beginning God created the heavens and the earth, not heaven and earth and hell. Still less is hell a place inhabited by Satan and his demons. In the book of Job, Satan is either talking to God in heaven or poking around on the earth. Paul wrote that the spiritual hosts of wickedness dwell in the heavenly places (Ephesians 6.12), and Revelation chapter 12 says that Satan and his angels will be in heaven, along with Michael and other angels, until Resurrection Day. The same chapter then says that after Resurrection Day Satan and his angels will be thrown out of heaven and come down to the earth. Nowhere does the Bible say that Satan inhabits a fiery place called hell.

So when Jesus says in Mark chapter 9, verses 47 and 48, *"And if your eye causes you to sin, pluck it out; it is better for you to enter the kingdom of God with one eye than with two eyes to be thrown into hell, where their worm does not die, and the fire is not quenched,"* the word translated as 'hell' is 'Gehenna', and he was simply saying, "It is better for you to enter the kingdom of God with one eye than with two eyes to be thrown on to the rubbish tip…"

With regard to the undying worm and unquenchable fire, Jesus was quoting the last verse of the book of the prophet Isaiah. God had been telling Isaiah what life would be like when Israel's enemies had finally been defeated. He concluded, *"And they shall go forth and look on the dead bodies of the men that have rebelled against me; for their worm shall not die, their fire shall not be quenched, and they shall be an abhorrence to all flesh."* (Isaiah 66.24) It's vital to see that this verse says the bodies of the rebellious men being consumed by worms and fire were dead bodies, not living bodies. There is no hint in this passage that the men who had rebelled against the Lord were somehow going to live in torment for ever, rather the opposite. The idea was that the worms wouldn't die and the fire wouldn't go out until the dead bodies had been entirely consumed.

Similarly, in Jeremiah 17.27 the Lord declared to the ancient Jews, *"…if you do not listen to me… then will I kindle a fire in* [Jerusalem's] *gates, and it shall devour the palaces of Jerusalem and shall not be quenched."* That prophecy of Jerusalem's destruction was fulfilled when the Babylonians torched the city. However, the fire they lit is not still burning today, so was the prophecy wrong? No. The Lord's word to Jeremiah never meant that the fire would burn for ever. It meant that no one would be able to quench its flames until they had completed their task of destruction.

It was these Old Testament pictures that Jesus was recalling in order to make his vivid point that it is better to make any sacrifice necessary to eliminate sin and enter the kingdom of God than to face the dreadful alternative of an ignominious, complete, final and permanent end to one's life from which there could be no escape.

It's true that Revelation chapters 19, 20 and 21 speak of a 'lake of fire', into which will be thrown Death, Hades, Satan and everyone whose name is not written in the book of life. However it's no more necessary to think that this will be a literal lake burning with fire than it is to think that the antichrist will be a beast with ten horns and seven heads as

Revelation 13.1 says he will be.[62] When Jesus warned his hearers that the unrighteous would be thrown into Gehenna he did not mean it literally. The Valley of Hinnom is probably no more than half a mile square, so there wouldn't be room in it for every unbeliever or wicked person who has ever lived to be burned up or eaten up there. Jesus used the word 'Gehenna' metaphorically, so John could equally have used the phrase 'the lake of fire' metaphorically. After all, you can't literally throw death anywhere, let alone into a lake, yet according to John death was thrown into the lake of fire. (Revelation 20.14) Throwing death into a lake of fire was merely a symbolical way of saying that death would come to an end, as indeed Revelation 21.4 says it will. So when John wrote that those whose names were not written in the book of life would follow Death and Hades into the lake of fire, he was saying in a symbolical way that they too would come to an end. The 'lake of fire' is a metaphor for a place of destruction. It doesn't have to be a real place at all.

The basis of judgement

(i) A matter of life or death

> *"I call heaven and earth to witness against*
> *you this day, that I have set before you life*
> *and death, blessing and curse; therefore choose*
> *life, that you and your descendants may live,*

---

[62] Some Bible commentators such as William Barclay take the view that the beast does not even symbolize a man, but the Roman Empire. That may have been John's intention, but even if it was I believe it will find a more significant fulfilment in the coming 'man of lawlessness' whom Paul spoke of in 2 Thessalonians 2.3.

loving the Lord your God, obeying his voice, and cleaving to him; for that means life to you and length of days, that you may dwell in the land which the Lord swore to your fathers, to Abraham, to Isaac, and to Jacob, to give them." (Deuteronomy 30.19,20)

'The wages of sin is death, but the free gift of God is eternal life in Christ Jesus our Lord.' (Romans 6.23)

In both the Old and the New Testaments God gives us a choice between life and death. In the Old Testament life meant a good life in this world; in the New Testament it means an even better life in the world to come. In both cases the alternative is death. The question for those who believe in Christ is, who gets to live for ever and who doesn't?

The passage from Deuteronomy actually gives us a clue. God wants to populate his eternal kingdom of righteousness with people who want to do his will because they love him. He doesn't want people who have to be forced to obey him, and he doesn't want people who refuse to obey him. He wants to have a gloriously happy world in which everyone loves him and everyone loves each other perfectly. And the reason he wants this is because that's how he loves us.

In the New Testament the passage from Romans tells us that God will freely grant eternal life to anyone who believes in Jesus for salvation and submits to Jesus as Lord. This is because through the work of the indwelling Holy Spirit Jesus can make us fit to live in the kingdom of God. (See Romans 8.1-4)

But what about people who want nothing to do with Jesus? Or people who have never even heard of him? How will their fate be decided? It depends on whether they are mules, wild boars, sheep or goats!

(ii) Mules

'And this is the judgement, that the light has come into the world, and men loved darkness rather than light, because their deeds were evil.' (John 3.19)

Through his Son Jesus Christ, God invites everyone to live for ever in his everlasting kingdom. And Jesus gave his life to make this possible. So how can anyone know this yet turn his back on Jesus? Anyone who knows about this amazing offer yet nevertheless rejects it is like a stubborn mule, a stubborn and tragically foolish mule. For God's word is unambiguous: *'He who believes in* [Jesus] *is not condemned; he who does not believe is condemned already, because he has not believed in the name of the only Son of God.'* (John 3.18) John wasn't writing about people who don't believe in Jesus because they have never heard of him: he meant people who do know about Jesus yet still refuse to believe in him. Unless they repent before they die, the verdict for them on the day of judgement has already been decided: it will be condemnation! Please, please don't be a mule!

(iii) Wild boars

Wild boars represent people who wilfully engage in all kinds of evil, who consistently oppose the will of God, and who live chiefly for themselves. Their behaviour is described in at least four places in the New Testament: Romans 1.29-31, 1 Corinthians 6.9-11, Galatians 5.19-21 and Ephesians 5.3-5.

Common sense tells us that a man who has raped innocent girls or gassed Jews or plundered a firm's assets before leaving it in bankruptcy is not likely to be granted citizenship in the kingdom of God. Jesus said, *"The Son of man will send his angels, and they will gather out of his kingdom all causes of sin and all evildoers, and throw them into the furnace of fire."* (Matthew 13.41,42) Unless such people truly repent before they die they won't inherit eternal life.

However the four references listed above include behaviour that seems to be far less serious. Some of it wouldn't be regarded as sin at all by many people. For example: gossiping, boasting and breaking promises; premarital sex, adultery and homosexual activities; greed, drunkenness, anger, jealousy; and even plain selfishness! God's word clearly states that continuing in any such behaviour will exclude us from his coming kingdom, and this even includes Christians! '*I warn you, as I warned you before, that those who do such things shall not inherit the kingdom of God,*' Paul wrote to the church in Galatia. (Galatians 5.21) '*Do not be deceived; neither the immoral... nor robbers will inherit the kingdom of God. And such were some of you. But you were washed, you were sanctified, you were justified* (made righteous) *in the name of the Lord Jesus Christ and in the Spirit of our God.*' (1 Corinthians 6.9,11) '*Let no one deceive you... it is because of these things that the wrath of God comes upon the sons of disobedience.*' (Ephesians 5.6)

Thankfully it's not a case of 'one strike and you're out'. The apostle Peter wasn't perfect, and Paul admitted that he wasn't. We don't have to be perfect, but we must *want* to be. Paul said that he was pressing on to perfection: he longed to be perfectly righteous through faith in Christ, and he was confident that eventually he would reach the goal he longed for. (Philippians 3.9-14; 2 Timothy 4.7,8) Our heavenly Father is seeking people who hunger and thirst after righteousness to live in his kingdom. (Matthew 4.6) Righteousness is simply living how God wants us to. If we don't want to live as he wants us to live, how can we expect the right to live in his kingdom of righteousness? After all, would *you* want to spend eternity surrounded by people who are selfish, rude, untruthful or even worse? We can't love God and at the same time want to continue in a lifestyle that he hates.

Where we find it hard to change, that is just where Jesus can help us. The very reason he came into the world was to deliver us from our sins, to make us fit to live in God's kingdom. '*...God is at work in you, both to will and to work for his good pleasure,*' Philippians 2.13 says. He does this through his Spirit living in us. '*...the fruit of the Spirit is love, joy, peace, patience, kindness, goodness, faithfulness, gentleness, self-control; against such there is no law.*' (Galatians 5.22,23) Jesus knows we can find it difficult to change, but he can change us if we'll let him. *"...if the Son makes you free, you will be free indeed."* (John 8.36)

So check out those four lists of unrighteous behaviour in Romans, Corinthians, Galatians and Ephesians. Agree with God's word. Ask Jesus to set you free from everything you read there that is hateful to God. Persist in prayer until you have the victory! Don't be a wild boar!

(iv) Sheep and goats

Sheep and goats stand for people who die never having heard of Jesus Christ, or with only a limited or distorted knowledge of him. They are not mules who have rejected his help, nor wild boars whose actions and lifestyle disqualify them from citizenship in the kingdom of God. They are simply people who have or have not loved their neighbours as themselves!

> *"When the Son of man comes in his glory, and all the angels with him, then he will sit on his glorious throne. Before him will be gathered all the nations, and he will separate them one from another as a shepherd separates the sheep from the goats, and he will place the sheep at his right hand, but the goats at the left. Then the King will say to those at his right hand, 'Come, O blessed of my Father, inherit the kingdom prepared for you from the foundation of the world; for I was hungry and you gave me food, I was thirsty and you gave me drink, I was a stranger and you welcomed me, I was naked and you clothed me, I was sick and you visited me, I was in prison and you came to me.' Then the righteous will answer him, 'Lord, when did we see thee hungry and feed thee, or thirsty and give thee drink? And when did we see thee a stranger and welcome thee, or naked and clothe thee? And when did we see thee sick or in prison and visit thee?' And the King will answer them, 'Truly, I say to you, as you did it to one*

of the least of these my brethren, you did it to me.' Then he will say to those at his left hand, 'Depart from me, you cursed, into the eternal fire prepared for the devil and his angels; for I was hungry and you gave me no food, I was thirsty and you gave me no drink, I was a stranger and you did not welcome me, naked and you did not clothe me, sick and in prison and you did not visit me.' Then they also will answer, 'Lord, when did we see thee hungry or thirsty or a stranger or naked or sick or in prison, and did not minister to thee?' Then he will answer them, 'Truly, I say to you, as you did it not to one of the least of these, you did it not to me.' And they will go away into eternal punishment, but the righteous into eternal life." (Matthew 25.31-46)

Some people understand Christ's 'brethren' in this passage to be Christians, people who have been born again as children of God and have thereby become Christ's brothers and sisters. But if that's so then people who had no contact with Christians could never qualify as sheep by helping them. The Bible commentator William Barclay understands the word 'brethren' differently. *'If we really wish to delight a parent's heart, if we really wish to move him to gratitude, the best way to do it is to help his child. God is the great Father; and the way to delight the heart of God is to help his children, our fellow men.'*[63]

---

[63] *The Gospel of Matthew, Volume 2.* W.Barclay, The Daily Study Bible, revised edition, The Saint Andrew Press, 1975, p.326.

The kind of help God is looking for is simple help that anyone can give. And it must not be motivated merely by the hope of a reward. Barclay continued, '*Those who helped did not think that they were helping Christ and thus piling up eternal merit… It was the natural, instinctive, quite uncalculating reaction of the loving heart. Whereas… the attitude of those who failed to help was, "If we had known it was you we would gladly have helped; but we thought it was only some common man who was not worth helping."*'

What a high bar this parable sets for people who haven't put their trust in Jesus for salvation! The goats will be condemned, not because of what they've done, but because of what they've not done.

Yet Jesus sets an even higher bar for those of us who *have* put our trust in him. *"A new commandment I give to you, that you love one another; even as I have loved you, that you also love one another,"* he said. (John 13.34) Thankfully by the grace of God our salvation in Christ is secure, but that must never lead us into complacency. Instead God's grace should motivate us 'to lead a life worthy of our calling', to aim for 'the measure of the stature of the fullness of Christ', and to 'press on to perfection'. (Ephesians 4.1; Ephesians 4.13; Philippians 3.12) Nothing less should satisfy us. (Matthew 5.6)

(v) The righteous judge

God has appointed his Son Jesus to be the judge, and his judgement will be totally just. (John 5.22; 2 Timothy 4.8)

- Jesus will take into account people's understanding of the Father's will. In a parable about disobedient servants Jesus said, *"...that servant who knew his master's will, but did not make ready or act according to his will, shall receive a severe beating. But he who did not know, and did what deserved a beating, shall receive a light beating."* (Luke 12.47,48)

- He will look at what people do rather than what they say. The son who did his father's will was the son who went to work in his father's vineyard even though he had said he wouldn't, rather than his brother who said he would go and then didn't. (Matthew 21.28-31)

- Yet he will look beyond what people do into their motivation. 1 Samuel 16.7 says, *"...man looks on the outward appearance, but the Lord looks on the heart."* A wealthy person who donates large sums to charity may look good to us but not to the Lord if his actions are motivated merely by the hope of gaining a peerage or senatorship. "Do you love me, Peter?" Jesus asked after Peter had badly let him down. In the end, what matters most is what's in our hearts.

(vi) Judgement by works?

In John 5.24 and John 5.21 Jesus declares that anyone who hears his teaching and believes it will not come in for judgement at all. *"Truly, truly, I say to you, he who hears my word and believes him who sent me, has eternal life; he does not come into judgment, but has* [already] *passed from death to life... For as the Father raises the dead and gives them life, so also the Son gives life to whom he will."* In other words, those who believe in Jesus have already begun a new life. They will be raised from the dead before the day of judgement comes and will then live for ever. This resurrection of believers is what Revelation 20.5 calls 'the first resurrection'.

Then in John 5.28,29 Jesus turns his attention to everyone else and the day of judgement. *"The hour is coming when all who are in the tombs* [and have not therefore been raised from the dead already] *will hear his voice and come forth, those who have done good, to the resurrection of life, and those who have done evil, to the resurrection of judgment."* Here Jesus is speaking of a second resurrection that will occur at the end of his thousand-year reign on the present earth. (See Revelation 20.5 again.) He says that this resurrection of everyone who has not believed in him will result in either *life* or *condemnation*. The word translated in verse 29 as 'judgement' can also mean 'condemnation', as in Hebrews 10.27. For these people judgement will not be on the basis of whether they have believed Jesus's teaching, for they may never have heard of him. It will be on the basis, Jesus says, of whether they have 'done good' or have 'done evil' during their lifetime. In other words, judgement for those who have not heard his teaching will be according to their works. This is confirmed in the description of Judgement Day given in Revelation 20.11-15:

> *… books were opened. Also another book was opened, which is the book of life. And the dead were judged by what was written in the books, by what they had done… all were judged by what they had done… and if anyone's name was not found written in the book of life, he was thrown into the lake of fire.*

Even the apostle Paul says that God *'will render to every man according to his works'*. (Romans 2.6) So why then does he say in Ephesians, *'...by grace you have been saved through faith; and this is not your own doing, it is the gift of God, <u>not</u> because of works, lest any man should boast'* (Ephesians 2.8,9)? It's because in his letter to the Ephesians Paul was addressing Christians, people who had heard the gospel and had put their faith in Jesus Christ. In the amazing love and grace of God, whatever we have done or have not done becomes irrelevant the moment we put our faith in Jesus to save us. Our works, whether good or bad, no longer count for or against us. We do not have to earn our citizenship in the kingdom of God. We have become God's sons and daughters, and as members of God's family citizenship is now ours by right. Praise the Lord!

Naturally this raises the question, "Can believers therefore be as wicked as they want without fear of condemnation?" In reality the question doesn't make sense because believers in Christ will not want to be wicked. The Bible says that people who truly accept Jesus as Saviour and Lord and live by the power of his Spirit will fulfil the requirements of God's law. They will love God and their neighbour and will no longer want to rebel against God's will:

> *For God has done what the law, weakened by the flesh, could not do:* [by] *sending his own Son in the likeness of sinful flesh and for sin, he condemned sin in the flesh, in order that the just requirement of the law might be fulfilled in us, who walk not according to the*

flesh but according to the Spirit. (Romans 8.3,4)

The fate of the unrighteous in the New Testament

So what will be the fate of the unrighteous? The New Testament mentions five different fates at Judgement Day for those who are not granted eternal life in the kingdom of God:

- Death, destruction or perishing (22 times)
- Gehenna, the Gehenna of fire, fire (26 times)
- Weeping and gnashing of teeth (7 times)
- Punishment (4 times)
- Torment (3 times)

We'll look at each of these in turn.

Death, destruction or perishing

(i) Death

The New Testament speaks of two deaths. The first death is when we die naturally. People who die as believers in Christ will then be resurrected on Resurrection Day. Their spirit will rejoin a resurrected and immortal body and they will never die again. Other people will be resurrected later on the day of judgement. On that day those who are not invited into God's kingdom will die a second time, but this time both their body and spirit will die. This is called the second death. It is the final end of life. *'Blessed and holy is he who shares in the first resurrection! Over such the second death has no power…'* (Revelation 20.6) Jesus described this second death as the death of body and soul. *"Do not fear those who kill the body but cannot kill the soul; rather fear him who can destroy both soul and body in hell."* (Matthew 10.28)

So when Paul wrote, *'…the wages of sin is death, but the free gift of God is eternal life in Christ Jesus…'* (Romans 6.23), he was writing about the second, final death. He was not writing about the first death, because even Christians have to die in body, at least until Resurrection Day is upon us. Jesus does not save us from the first death, but he will save us from the second death by grace, if we truly trust in him as our saviour and Lord.

(ii) Destruction

In the Authorized Version of the Bible the English words 'destroy', 'destroyed' or 'destroying' occur about *500 times*, and they always mean the annihilation of whatever is destroyed, not its continuing existence. So when these words are applied to the final destiny of the ungodly, that is just what they must mean: their annihilation. We must not change the meaning of a word just because we'd prefer it to mean something else.

Jesus Christ said we must choose between the way to life and the way to destruction:

> *"Enter by the narrow gate; for the gate is wide*
> *and the way is easy, that leads to destruction,*
> *and those who enter by it are many. For the*

> *gate is narrow and the way is hard, that*
> *leads to life, and those who find it are few."*
> (Matthew 7.13,14)

When he said, *"Do not fear those who kill the body but cannot kill the soul; rather fear him who can destroy both soul and body in hell"* he was saying that men can *kill* us (*apokteinai*) but God can *destroy* us (*apolesai*). *Apolesai* is stronger than *apokteinai*. According to the authoritative Grimm-Thayer Greek-English lexicon, *apolesai* means 'to destroy, i.e. to put out of the way entirely, abolish, put an end to, ruin'. So Jesus was saying that while men can merely kill the body in the first death, God can destroy both the body and soul in the second death, bringing us to an end entirely. Both are cases of destruction, but God's destruction will be complete destruction.

Peter uses a different Greek word for destruction in 2 Peter 3.7: '...*the heavens and earth that now exist have been stored up for fire, being kept until the day of judgement and destruction of ungodly men.*' Here the word for destruction, *apōleias*, means 'the destroying or utter destruction of something or someone'. Peter says that the destiny of ungodly men is to be utterly destroyed.

In 2 Thessalonians 1.5-9 Paul writes about what he calls '...*the righteous judgement of God... when the Lord Jesus is revealed from heaven with his mighty angels in flaming fire, inflicting vengeance upon those who do not know God and upon those who do not obey the Gospel of our Lord Jesus. They shall suffer* (pay) *the punishment of eternal destruction and exclusion from* (away from) *the presence of the Lord and from the glory of his might.*' Here Paul uses another

Greek word for 'destruction', but it means much the same as the others. *Olethros* means 'ruin, destruction, death'. Paul unambiguously states that the coming vengeance and punishment for the ungodly will be eternal and permanent 'ruin, destruction and death'.

Destruction means destruction. None of these verses suggests everlasting existence, punishment or torment. What awaits the ungodly at the day of judgement is not everlasting punishment but permanent destruction. It couldn't be clearer that the alternative to eternal life is to perish, to be blotted out, to be utterly destroyed, to cease to exist for ever.

(iii) Perishing

The other word use for the destiny of the ungodly is 'perish'. John 3.16, possibly the most famous verse in the Bible, presents everyone with a choice between eternal life and perishing. '*For God so loved the world that he gave his only Son, that whoever believes in him should not perish but have eternal life.*' According to the lexicon, the Greek word used in this verse for 'perish', *apolētai*, means 'to destroy, i.e. to put out of the way entirely, abolish, put an end to, ruin'. The same word is used many times in the New Testament. Old wineskins 'perish', the world as it was first created 'perished' in the Flood, the disciples thought they would 'perish' in a storm on the Sea of Galilee, those who take the sword will 'perish' by the sword. In every case 'perish' means to come to an end, to be destroyed, to die. So John 3.16 says that people who do not receive eternal life will come to an end, be destroyed, die. There is not the slightest suggestion that they will continue to live for ever, still less in torment.

(iv) Immortal souls?

Some people believe that our souls are immortal, which means by definition that they cannot die. If our souls really were immortal then even God could not destroy them, any more than he could make a four-sided triangle or a foot ruler that's three-feet long. But the idea that our souls are immortal comes from Plato and other ancient Greek philosophers, not the Bible. The Bible does say that God 'has put eternity into man's mind' (Ecclesiastes 3.11) but all that means is that we have an innate sense that we were meant to live for ever. Jesus said, *"…do not fear those* (i.e. men) *who kill the body but cannot kill the soul; rather fear him* (i.e. God) *who can destroy both body <u>and soul</u> in hell* (Gehenna).*"* (Matthew 10.28)

Gehenna, the Gehenna of fire, fire

Jesus frequently said that the ungodly would be cast into Gehenna or into eternal fire.

> *"…if your right hand causes you to sin, cut it off and throw it away; it is better that you lose one of your members than that your whole body go into hell* (Gehenna).*"* (Matthew 5.30)

> *"…if your eye causes you to sin, pluck it out and throw it away; it is better for you to*

> *enter life with one eye than with two eyes to*
> *be thrown into the hell* (Gehenna) *of fire."*
> (Matthew 18.9)

> *"...if your hand or foot causes you to sin, cut*
> *it off and throw it away; it is better for you*
> *to enter life maimed or lame than with two*
> *hands or two feet to be thrown into the eternal*
> *fire."* (Matthew 18.8)

John the Baptist employed the concept of fire too: *"...*
he will clear his threshing floor and gather his wheat into
the granary, but the chaff he will burn with unquenchable
fire." (Matthew 3.12) And in the last chapter of the Old
Testament, the prophet Malachi leaves us in no doubt that
the fire of God's judgement will bring the life of evildoers
to a complete end. No part of them will survive:

> *"For behold, the day comes, burning like an*
> *oven, when all the arrogant and all evildoers*
> *will be stubble; the day that comes shall*
> *burn them up, says the Lord of hosts, so that*
> *it will leave them neither root nor branch."*
> (Malachi 4.4)

Just as the rubbish tip in the Valley of Hinnom was a
place for getting rid of refuse, so a fire is the ultimate way
of destroying something. In earlier centuries when nearly
all homes were heated by coal fires, anything that could
burn would be thrown into the fire to destroy it. If a woman
received an unwanted circular she would throw it in the
fire. If a man wrote a new will and asked what he should do

with the old one he would be told, "Throw it in the fire". That is what people always did when they needed to destroy something; when they wanted to be certain that it did not continue to exist.

Wherever the Bible tells us that the ungodly will be cast into Gehenna or eternal fire it means that their destiny is to be destroyed.

Weeping and gnashing of teeth

On six occasions in Matthew's Gospel and once in Luke's Gospel Jesus prophesies that evildoers will weep and gnash their teeth when they meet their doom.

For example, *"…many will come from east and west and sit at table with Abraham, Isaac, and Jacob in the kingdom of heaven, while the sons of the kingdom will be thrown into the outer darkness; there men will weep and gnash their teeth."* (Matthew 8.11,12)

Weeping is an expression of grief. Teeth gnashing is always associated in the Old Testament with anger or hatred. It's not obvious whether the anger or hatred of the teeth-gnashers will be directed at God for excluding them from his kingdom, or at themselves for being so foolish as to ignore God and his will and thereby forfeit eternal life, but I think it will be the latter. In other words, they will be stricken with grief and remorse.

There is a long description of such remorse in the *Wisdom of Solomon*, a Jewish book written around the time of Jesus. The passage begins, '*When the unrighteous see* [the righteous in bliss]*, they will be shaken with dreadful fear, and they will be amazed at the unexpected salvation of the righteous. They will* *speak to one another in repentance, and in anguish of spirit they will groan, and say, "These are persons whom we once held in derision and made a byword of reproach – fools that we were!"* (Wisdom of Solomon 5.1-5) Another Jewish book of that time, 2 Esdras, says that there will be a week's delay after judgement, which will give the wicked an opportunity to reflect on their wrongdoing and their consequent loss of eternal life, as well as for the righteous to rejoice! (2 Esdras 7.101)

So it may be that at the last judgement those whose names are not found in the book of life will be given time to reflect on their folly in ignoring God, in living selfishly, in doing bad things and in not believing the truth. When they realize that God really is going to make a new and perfect earth in which they could have lived for ever, then truly they will weep and gnash their teeth.

As I said at the beginning, many Christians assume that this will continue for ever in hell. But it is not obvious from any of these passages how long the weeping and teeth gnashing will last, nor where it will take place. Not one of these passages says that it will continue for ever. Although Jesus repeatedly uses the word 'there', in three cases it is in 'the outer darkness', twice in 'the furnace of fire', once 'with the hypocrites', and once somewhere away from Jesus and excluded from the kingdom of God. These differences in location suggest that Jesus did not intend the various expressions of location to be understood literally. Job 18.18 and Job 8.13 in the Authorized Version show that 'outer darkness' and 'with the hypocrites' were simply expressions for separation from God. 'The furnace' was a metaphor for destruction, set in the context of a parable about harvest time. In Matthew 13.40-42 the destination of evildoers was in 'the furnace of fire' because that is where weeds were put. *"Just as the weeds are gathered and burned with fire, so will it be at the close of the age. ...they will gather out of his kingdom all causes of sin and all evildoers, and throw them into the furnace of fire; there men will weep and gnash their teeth."* (Evidently farmers in the first century weren't concerned about global warming!)

Nevertheless people commonly equate the phrases 'outer darkness', 'with the hypocrites', 'the furnace of fire' and 'thrust out of the kingdom' with the traditional idea of hell. They conclude that the wicked will continue to weep and gnash their teeth in some kind of fire for ever. They come to this conclusion in spite of the fact that Jesus said the alternative to eternal life is to *perish* (John 3.16), and that after the day of judgement and the creation of a new heaven and earth *everything* that remains will be united in and with Christ. (Revelation 21.4; Ephesians 1.10) That can never be true if most people will continue to exist in an everlasting state of remorse, separated from Christ. So what did Jesus mean by 'there'?

All seven of these passages are principally about the coming separation of 'good' and 'bad' people at the end of this age, and about the grief and remorse the 'bad' people will experience on learning that they have been excluded from the kingdom of God. Instead of being invited to sit at table in the kingdom of God they are thrust outside; instead of being gathered into the barn they are burned outside in a furnace; instead of being put into vessels for use as good fish they are thrown back into the sea; instead of being invited into the house they are shut out of it; instead of being a guest at a wedding feast they are thrown out into the night. Their remorse is not because of where they end up, which Jesus left deliberately vague. They are not weeping because everything outside is dark. They are not grinding their teeth because of burning flames. Their remorse is because of where they have *not* ended up, i.e. in the kingdom of God! The passage in Luke's Gospel makes this particularly clear: *"When once the householder has risen up and shut the door, you will begin to stand outside and to knock at the door, saying, 'Lord, open to us.' … But he will say, 'I tell you, I do not know where you come from; depart from me, all you workers of iniquity!' There you will weep and gnash your teeth, when you see Abraham and Isaac and Jacob and all the prophets in the kingdom of God and you yourselves thrust out."* (Luke 13.25-28)

The decision to exclude the unrighteous from the kingdom of God will be announced at the judgement seat of Christ. (Matthew 25.31,32; Revelation 20.11-13). It is *there* that the unrighteous will learn their fate, so it is *there* that they will weep and gnash their teeth in consequence.

All we can say with confidence from these seven passages about teeth and tears is that at the day of judgement evildoers will bitterly regret the life they have led when they discover that they are to be excluded from everlasting life in the kingdom of God. That is the essence of what Jesus was teaching. And he did this in order to urge his hearers – and all of us who read his words today – not to end up in that same terrible state when we discover that everything Jesus taught really was true; and that because we ignored his teaching and left God out of our lives we have irrevocably forfeited the possibility of living for ever in a world beyond our wildest dreams, but instead we shall be destroyed like weeds in a furnace.

It was out of love for you and me that Jesus issued these dire warnings. Charles Wesley expressed this in a hymn[64] addressed to anyone who has not yet asked Jesus to be his saviour. The words are based on Ezekiel 33.11:

> *Sinners turn; why will ye die? God, your Maker, asks you why.*
> *God, who did your being give, made you with Himself to live,*
> *He the fatal cause demands, asks the work of His own hands:*
> *Why, ye reckless creatures, why will you cross His love, and die?*
>
> Charles Wesley

Punishment

(i) Matthew 25.46

In Matthew 25.46, Jesus ended his teaching on the last judgement by describing the fate of the 'goats'. *"And they will go away into eternal punishment, but the righteous into eternal life."* In the Authorized Version the fate of the goats sounds even worse: *"And these shall go away into <u>everlasting</u> punishment: but the righteous into life eternal."*

At first sight the word 'everlasting' seems to contradict the fact that the alternative to eternal life is, as we have seen, to perish. (John 3.16) How can anyone perish everlastingly? *Aiōnios*, the word that is translated in the Authorized

---

[64] Hymn no. 327 in *The Methodist Hymnbook*, Methodist Conference Office, London, 1933.

Version as both 'eternal' and 'everlasting', has several possible meanings. It is the adjective from the noun *aiōn*. (The English version of this is 'aeon'.) *Aiōn* can mean 'life and breath, a human lifetime, an unbroken age, a historical age, the age or ages to come, perpetuity of time, or eternity past present and future'. So *aiōnios* can mean 'everlasting', but it can equally mean 'the kind that will exist in the age to come' or even 'permanent'. In Matthew 10.28 Jesus said that the punishment awaiting sinners will be the destruction of both their bodies and souls. In other words, it will be a final death from which there can be no resurrection, an eternal death as distinct from a temporal death, the permanent kind of death that will exist in the age to come, not the mere physical death of the body which will be brought back to life to face judgement. And that is why Jesus described the forthcoming punishment of the unrighteous as eternal.

Precisely the same point is made in *The New Bible Commentary Revised*[65]: '*Eternal punishment* and *eternal life* are not necessarily the same in duration. *Eternal* (Gk. *aiōnios*) simply refers to the age to come and makes the point that the division is final for men's destiny.'

(ii) 2 Thessalonians 1.8,9

'*...those who do not know God and those who do not obey the gospel of our Lord Jesus...shall suffer* (pay) *the punishment of eternal destruction and exclusion from the presence of the Lord...*' (2 Thessalonians 1.8,9) Here Paul clarifies what Jesus meant by punishment in Matthew 25.46. It will be

---

[65] *The New Bible Commentary Revised*. D.Guthrie and others. Inter-Varsity Press, Leicester, 1970, p.846.

destruction, the final destruction of the ungodly and their resulting permanent exclusion from the Lord's presence.

(iii) 2 Peter 2.9

'...the Lord knows how to rescue the godly from trial, and to keep the unrighteous under punishment until the day of judgement...' (2 Peter 2.9)

As it is translated in the Revised Standard Version this verse is rather confusing. Why will God punish anyone before the day of judgement comes? The Greek word *kolazomenous*, translated as 'under punishment', can equally well be translated as 'under restraint'. That is how it should be translated here, as well as in Acts 4.21, where the chief concern of the Jewish rulers was not to punish Peter and John, but to curb or restrain them from preaching the gospel.

(iv) Hebrews 10.28,29

'A man who has violated the law of Moses dies without mercy at the testimony of two or three witnesses. How much worse punishment do you think will be deserved by the man who has spurned the Son of God...' (Hebrews 10.28,29)

This is the final verse in the New Testament that speaks of 'punishment' following the day of judgement. But once again the punishment spoken of is destruction rather than some perpetual torment. The writer is talking about believers in Christ who deliberately turn their back on him and actually become adversaries to the Christian faith. In the two previous verses he (or she) describes what their punishment will be: 'For if we sin deliberately after receiving the knowledge of the truth, there no longer remains a sacrifice *for sins, but a fearful prospect of judgement, and a fury of fire which will <u>consume</u> the adversaries.'*

(v) The painful scales of justice

There are two final questions about punishment that need answering. Will the destined destruction of the ungodly be painful, and if so will it be equally painful for everyone?

A child's instinctive cry, "It's not fair," arises from a conviction we all have that injustice is wrong. The other day I was reading about a massacre that took place in the Kandhamal district of eastern India in August 2008. Hindu nationalists murdered more than 90 Christians. 5,600 houses were looted and burned, and some 295 churches and other places of worship were destroyed. Yet in spite of over 3,300 complaints to the police almost 90% of the known perpetrators were acquitted. Every molecule of morality and corpuscle of conscience screams out that this was wrong; that at the very least the perpetrators should have been brought to justice and punished. To allow them to pursue their normal life scot-free, Hindu-free or any other kind of free while most of their innocent victims continue to suffer without compensation is undeniably "not fair".

In contrast, the Bible tells us that the Lord God *is* fair: he will do what is right. *"Shall not the Judge of all the earth do right?"* asked Abraham, and the Lord evidently agreed with him. (Genesis 18.25) As the righteous judge, the Lord assures us that either in this life or the next he will repay wrongdoing. *"Vengeance is mine: I will repay, says the Lord."* (Romans 12.19)

The principle that God laid down for justice on earth

was that wrongdoing must be punished, and that it must be punished in proportion to the wrongdoing itself:

> *He who kills a man shall be put to death. He who kills a beast shall make it good, life for life. When a man causes a disfigurement in his neighbour, as he has done it shall be done to him, fracture for fracture, eye for eye, tooth for tooth. As he has disfigured a man, he shall be disfigured.* (Leviticus 24.17-20)

The idea that the punishment should fit the crime may sound barbarous in our gentler culture, but imagine how merciful it would have sounded only a few centuries ago when a man could be hanged just for stealing a lamb! If then the Lord is going to be true to his own principle of punishing wrongdoers in proportion to their crimes, how could he make all evildoers suffer exactly the same fate at the day of judgement, particularly if that fate were merely to bring their lives to a quiet and peaceful end? How could it be just for men like Stalin, Hitler, Ivan the Terrible, Vlad the Impaler and others like them to suffer exactly the same fate on Judgement Day as a little old lady who has merely lived rather selfishly?

We have already seen that the unrighteous will experience a period of remorse before their final destruction. But the Bible goes further than this. Its unchanging image of the means of that final destruction is the image of fire. (See Malachai 4.1; Matthew 3.12 & 13.40,41; 2 Peter 3.7-10; Revelation 20.15.) Being burnt to death doesn't take for ever but it doesn't happen instantaneously either, and furthermore it is extremely painful. So while the Bible firmly declares that the destiny of the damned is their final extinction, I believe that prior to this they will have to suffer in proportion to the suffering that they themselves have inflicted.

This is surely what Paul was writing about in 2 Thessalonians 1.5-8:

> *This is evidence of the righteous judgment of God, that you may be made worthy of the kingdom of God, for which you are suffering — since indeed God deems it just to repay with affliction those who afflict you, and to grant rest with us to you who are afflicted, when the Lord Jesus is revealed from heaven with his mighty angels in flaming fire, inflicting vengeance upon those who do not know God and upon those who do not obey the gospel of our Lord Jesus.*

I know that God is merciful and kind, and that *'he does not willingly afflict or grieve the sons of men.'* (Lamentations 3.33) Nevertheless that is exactly what he does do when it is necessary for the sake of justice. He destroyed all but eight inhabitants of Sodom and Gomorrah with fire and brimstone, and all but eight inhabitants of the earth with a universal flood. Following the world-wide evacuation of believers in Christ on Resurrection Day, Revelation chapter 16 tells us that God is going to pour out his wrath on those who remain during the last three and a half years before Christ returns. If those remaining inhabitants of the earth are to suffer foul sores, scorching heat and hailstones weighing a hundredweight, how could it be just for men and women who lived earlier in history like Paul Pot who caused the death of a third of Cambodia's population to be rewarded on the day of judgement with nothing worse than a quick and painless end?

So the all-important question arises: did Jesus himself support the idea that wrongdoers will be punished in proportion to their guilt? Absolutely!

> *"Woe to you, Chorazin! Woe to you, Beth-saida! For if the mighty works done in you had been done in Tyre and Sidon, they would have repented long ago in sackcloth and ashes. But I tell you, it shall be more tolerable on the day of judgment for Tyre and Sidon than for you."* (Matthew 11.21,22)

> *"That servant who knew his master's will, but did not make ready or act according to his will, shall receive a severe beating. But he who did not know, and did what deserved a beating, shall receive a light beating."* (Luke 12.47,48)

It is only my fancy, but if the fires of God's judgement have to destroy the evil in men's hearts as well as their bodies and souls, it may necessarily take longer to burn them up if their deeds have been especially evil. I presume that the longer it takes the more painful their destruction will be.

(vi) Conclusion

The word 'punishment' in connection with the final destiny of the damned is mentioned only four times in the New Testament. It is defined as their destruction or their consumption by fire. Where it is described as 'eternal' it means that it will be permanent and final: the resulting death of the unrighteous will include their total destruction, body and soul.

God is love. He loves every single person he has made. He is neither vindictive nor cruel. The kindest, most loving thing he can do for people who don't want to live under the lordship of Jesus his Son is to bring their life to an end, and that is what he will do. But before doing that he will rectify every injustice that has not already been taken care of on earth. This will take the form of punishment in proportion to whatever evil has been committed. How long this will last is not stated, but it has to end before the creation of the new earth, when pain and death will be no more. (Revelation 21.1-4) Of one thing we can be sure: it will last no longer and be no worse than necessary.

On the day of judgement the requirements of justice will be fully satisfied, just as they are on earth today whenever just rulers carry out their responsibilities properly.

Torment

Nevertheless, there are three passages in the New Testament which seem to say that the wicked, or at least some of them, will be everlastingly tormented, beginning either after their first death or after the day of judgement.

(i) The rich man and Lazarus

In Luke chapter 16 Jesus told a story about an unnamed rich man and a very poor man named Lazarus who both died at about the same time. Here is part of the story:

> *"The rich man also died and was buried; and in Hades, being in torment, he lifted up his eyes, and saw Abraham far off and Lazarus in his bosom. And he called out, 'Father Abraham, have mercy upon me, and send Lazarus to dip the end of his finger in water and cool my tongue; for I am in anguish in this flame. …send him to my father's house, for I have five brothers, so that he may warn them, lest they also come into this place of torment.' But Abraham said, 'They have Moses and the prophets; let them hear them.'"*
> (Luke 16.22-29)

This story is rather strange:

• It is the only passage in the Bible that represents Hades or Sheol as a place of flames and torment. As we have seen, Job wrote, '*There the wicked cease from troubling, and there the weary are at rest. There the prisoners are at ease together.*' (Job 3.17,18) Other passages in the Old Testament tell us that there is no knowledge there, no remembrance of God or anything else, and no speaking. (Ecclesiastes 9.10; Psalm 88.11,12) If Jesus meant this parable to be taken literally he would have been contradicting the word of God in the Old Testament. And nowhere else does Jesus himself describe Hades as a place of torment or even warn his hearers against ending up there.

- When Jesus told this parable everybody, rich and poor alike, went in spirit to Hades at their death, even the prophet Samuel. (Job 3.19; 1 Samuel 28.3-19) So why did Lazarus go somewhere nicer?

- In the Bible the dead are always regarded as sleeping, i.e. unconscious, until they are resurrected on Resurrection Day or at the last judgement. (Daniel 12.2; Matthew 9.24; 1 Corinthians 15.18; 1 Thessalonians 4.13-17) Yet as soon as the rich man died he and Abraham were conversing with each other.

- It suggests that Lazarus went to a place of blessing simply because he was poor.

- By describing the rich man as being in torment while his brothers are still alive, it suggests that judgement takes place the moment someone dies. However, the New Testament consistently says that the destiny of people who do not believe in Jesus won't be decided until the day of judgement.

- It suggests that disembodied souls have eyes, fingers and tongues!

The explanation is simply that it was a story Jesus made up, based on the beliefs of the Pharisees whom he was addressing. Almost every detail of this story can be found in Jewish writings in the Talmud and other literature current at the time. For example, in the Babylonian Talmud, Book II, folio 72, 'Kiddushin', it is said of a rabbi on the day of his death, "This day he sits in Abraham's bosom." Jesus told this story in terms that the Pharisees could accept in order to show them truths that they were not accepting. The Sadducees once did exactly the same thing to Jesus. They didn't believe in any resurrection, but they told Jesus a fictional story about a woman who had seven husbands in turn, and then asked him whose wife she would be in 'the resurrection'. Just as they made up a story in terms of something they didn't personally believe, in order to get their point over to Jesus, so Jesus made up a story about the rich man and Lazarus in terms that he didn't believe, in order to get his point over to the Pharisees in terms that they could accept. Jesus told this story primarily to urge his audience to believe the teaching of Moses and the prophets, and to tell them that if they didn't do so then even when he rose from the dead they would not believe in him. He never intended it to be a factual account of what happens in the afterlife.

Sadly this parable has been influential in shaping an understanding of life immediately after death that is contrary to the Bible's teaching, including the false doctrine of purgatory.

(ii) Revelation 14.9-11

> *"If any one worships the beast and its image, and receives a mark on his forehead or on his hand, he also shall drink the wine of God's wrath, poured unmixed into the cup of his anger, and he shall be tormented with fire and sulphur in the presence of the holy angels and in the presence of the Lamb. And the*

> *smoke of their torment goes up for ever and*
> *ever; and they have no rest, day or night,*
> *these worshippers of the beast and its image,*
> *and whoever receives the mark of its name."*
> (Revelation 14.9-11)

These verses describe the fate of people who surrender to the antichrist during the last three and a half years, not the fate of anyone who dies before then. We are told that those who worship the beast will be tormented with fire and sulphur by a wrathful God in the presence of Jesus and his angels; 'the smoke of their torment' will continue 'for ever and ever', and that they 'have no rest, day or night'. To understand all this we first have to understand how the various words and phrases are used elsewhere in the Bible:

- The Greek word *basanizō*, translated 'torment', normally means 'to vex with grievous pains of body or mind, to torment'. However in Revelation 18.9,10,15-17 John uses the same word 'torment' to refer to the destruction of Rome. (Revelation 17.1-12 makes it clear 'Babylon' is a pseudonym for the city of Rome. If John had openly encouraged people to except the imminent destruction of Rome he could easily have been put to death as a traitor.) *'And the kings of the earth... will weep and wail over her when they see the smoke of her burning; they will stand far off, in fear of her <u>torment</u>... The merchants... will stand far off, in fear of her <u>torment,</u> weeping and mourning aloud, "Alas, alas, for the great city... In one hour all this wealth has been laid waste."'*

So in Revelation the word 'torment' can refer to a relatively brief process of destruction.

- 'Fire and sulphur (brimstone)' is an expression used in the Bible for a principal means of destruction used by the Lord. '*Then the Lord rained on Sodom and Gomorrah brimstone and fire from the Lord out of heaven; and he overthrew those cities, and all the valley, and all the inhabitants of the cities...*' (Genesis 19.24,25) '*On the wicked* [the Lord] *will rain coals of fire and brimstone...*' (Psalm 11.6) '*And the streams of Edom shall be turned into pitch, and her soil into brimstone; her land shall become burning pitch.*' (Isaiah 34.9) '*...the heads of the horses were like lions' heads, and fire and smoke and sulphur issued from their mouths. By these three plagues a third of mankind was killed, by the fire and smoke and sulphur issuing from their mouths.*' (Revelation 9.17,18) The Lord sends fire and brimstone to produce destruction and death.

- The Greek word *orgē*, translated 'wrath', is used in the New Testament to mean 'God's anger at man's disobedience, obduracy (especially in resisting the gospel) and sin, which expresses itself in punishing the sinner'.[66] An earthly ruler acts on God's behalf in punishing wrongdoers: '*...he does not bear the sword in vain; he is the servant of God to execute his wrath on the wrongdoer.*' (Romans 13.4) In the Bible any ruler

---

[66] *A Greek-English lexicon of the New Testament.* Grimm's Wilke's Clavis Novi Testamenti, translated, revised and enlarged by Joseph H. Thayer, fourth edition, T & T Clark, Edinburgh, 1901.

who did not punish the wicked would be regarded as a bad ruler who encouraged wrongdoing.

- 'The smoke of their torment will continue for ever' is a Biblical expression that means the associated destruction will be permanent. It may also contain the idea that the destruction will be permanently remembered. Prophesying the forthcoming destruction of the land of Edom, Isaiah wrote, '... *its smoke shall go up for ever. From generation to generation it shall lie waste; none shall pass through it for ever and ever.*' (Isaiah 34.10,11) Clearly Edom did not burn for ever and the smoke of its burning did not go up for ever, but its destruction lasted for ever: it was a permanent destruction. In Revelation 19.3 a multitude in heaven celebrates the burning of Rome (see Revelation 18.8) with the words, *"Hallelujah! The smoke from her goes up for ever and ever!"* This did not literally mean that the smoke would rise for ever, for two chapters later John tells us that Rome and everything else in the present earth will pass away and God will make all things new. (Revelation 21.1,5) The heavenly multitude probably meant that the destruction of Rome would never be forgotten.

- The Greek word *anapausin*, translated 'rest', means 'intermission', 'cessation', 'rest' or 'recreation'.

- 'Day *and* night' is a phrase used in the Bible to mean 'continuously'. *"This book of the law shall not depart from your mouth, but you shall meditate on it day and night..."* (Joshua 1.8) '...*his delight is in the law of the Lord, and on his law he meditates day and night.'* (Psalm 1.2) At the dedication of the temple Solomon prayed *"...that thy eyes may be open day and night toward this house..."* (2 Chronicles 6.20) 'Day and night' always means something that happens or is done continuously. (See also Psalms 32.4; 42.3; 55.10; 88.1.)

- 'Day *or* night' and 'day *nor* night' are phrases used in the Bible to refer to something that does *not* happen or is *not* done. *'...neither day nor night one's eyes see sleep...'* (Ecclesiastes 8.16) *"...neither eat nor drink for three days, night or day."* (Esther 4.16) *'It shall not be quenched night nor day...'* (Isaiah 34.10 AV. 'Nor' is the correct translation of this verse in Isaiah, not 'and' as in the RSV.)

These verses in Revelation 14.9-11 cannot mean that those who worship the beast will be tortured in flames for ever in the presence of the Lamb, for the Lamb is Jesus, and when Jesus comes to dwell on earth in the heavenly city, there will be no more crying nor pain in his presence (Revelation 21.4,22,23), and nothing and no one will be accursed any more. (Revelation 22.3) Here are some further reasons:

- <u>Destruction</u> As we have seen earlier, the fate of the damned is the permanent destruction of body and soul; it is not eternal life in any form. *'The wages of sin is death.'* (Romans 6.23)
- <u>Everlasting joy</u> To those whose names are written in the book of life God has promised to wipe every tear from their eyes, and that sorrow and sighing

will be replaced by everlasting joy. (Revelation 21.4; Isaiah 35.10) How could they be free from sorrow and sighing if they knew that unbelieving members of their families – perhaps even their own children – were everlastingly burning to death in flames of choking sulphur?[67]

- <u>Vengeance</u> God has said, *"Vengeance is mine; I will repay,"* (Deuteronomy 32.35; Romans 12.19; Hebrews 10.30). God said this to stop people taking vengeance into their own hands, by promising that he would deal with wrongdoers himself. In 2 Thessalonians 1.5-9 Paul does indeed state that the Lord Jesus will inflict 'vengeance upon those who do not know God and upon those who do not obey the gospel of our Lord Jesus', but he immediately explains what form that vengeance will take: '*They shall suffer the punishment of eternal destruction*.' The Greek words *olethron aiōnion* mean their permanent ruin, destruction or death. That is the principal vengeance that God will inflict on the disobedient, through his Son Jesus.

- <u>Justice</u> *"...all his ways are justice. ...just and right is he."* (Deuteronomy 32.4) God himself laid down a rule that justice must be equitable: 'an eye for an eye and a tooth for a tooth'. (See Leviticus 24.17-20) How then could he torment for ever someone who has been forced into worshipping an idol for

---

[67] As I deduce in Chapter 11, there will be weeks and months in the age to come, so it would not be true to argue that there is no time in eternity.

no more than three and a half years in order to buy food for this children?

- <u>Anger</u> God's anger against sinners will not last for ever. *'He will not always chide, nor will he keep his anger for ever.'* (Psalm 103.8,9)
- <u>Mercy</u> God is merciful. *"Be merciful, even as your Father is merciful."* (Luke 6.36) Everlasting torture would by definition be unmerciful.

So what *do* these verses in Revelation mean?

Using the explanations I have given above, the words, *"he also shall drink the wine of God's wrath, poured unmixed into the cup of his anger, and he shall be tormented with fire and sulphur in the presence of the holy angels and in the presence of the Lamb. And the smoke of their torment goes up for ever and ever"* mean that anyone who worships the beast will be justly and permanently destroyed by God in the presence of Jesus.

The second part, *"and they have no rest, day or night, these worshippers of the beast and its image and whoever receives the mark of its name,"* has to be correctly translated and punctuated in order to be understood. Although the RSV says 'day or night', the Greek says 'day *and* night'. As I've explained, 'day and night' always means something that happens or is done continuously, not something that doesn't happen, like not having any rest. Secondly, there was no punctuation in the original Greek text, so we have to decide from the context where one sentence ends and another begins. Although this second part begins with the word 'and', John begins at least half the sentences in this chapter with the word 'and', so it could easily be the start of another separate sentence. It would then literally be translated, '(And) they have no cessation day and night the ones worshipping the beast and its image and if anyone receives the mark of its name.' This new sentence is now a comment on the previous sentence. It explains that God's condemnation and sentence of death on these people is just because day and night without ceasing they worship the beast and its image. Their behaviour is the antithesis of the behaviour of the four living creatures around the throne of God in Revelation chapter 5. The four heavenly creatures never cease day and night to worship God! '*…day and night they never cease to sing, "Holy, holy, holy, is the Lord God Almighty, who was and is and is to come!"'* (Revelation 4.8)[68]

So this second part of Revelation 14.9-11 is not about ceaseless torment, it is about the ceaseless worship of the beast worshippers, which justifies their death sentence.

(iii) Revelation 20.9,10

The third passage in the New Testament about torment is in Revelation chapter 20. Two verses describe the fate of the human armies of the antichrist who will assemble to attack Jerusalem at the end of Christ's thousand-year reign, and the fate of the antichrist, the false prophet and the devil.

> *And they marched up over the broad earth*
> *and surrounded the camp of the saints and the*

---

[68] The Greek of Revelation 4.8 says, 'They do not have respite day and night they are saying holy, holy, holy' etc. The phrase 'day and night' describes what they *are* doing, not what they are *not* doing, just as it does in other Bible passages.

> *beloved city; but fire came down from heaven and consumed them, and the devil who had deceived them was thrown into the lake of fire and sulphur where the beast and the false prophet were, and they will be tormented day and night for ever and ever.* (Revelation 20.9,10)

The most obvious meaning of these verses from the Revised Standard Version is that the human armies of the antichrist, together with the antichrist, the false prophet and the devil, will be tormented for ever in a lake of fire and sulphur. This presents two further problems.

Firstly, verse 9 says that the human armies will be consumed by fire. The Greek word translated 'consume', *katefagen*, means 'to consume by eating, to eat up, to devour; or to utterly consume or destroy by fire'. That can only mean the end of them. This contradicts verse 10, which seems to say they will then be tormented day and night for ever and ever. Happily there is a simple solution to this problem. As I said, the Greek text itself doesn't have any punctuation, and John often starts a sentence in Revelation with the word 'and'. So without changing any words, the two verses above should be punctuated as two separate sentences like this: *'And they marched up over the broad earth and surrounded the camp of the saints and the beloved city; but fire came down from heaven and consumed them. And the devil who had deceived them was thrown into the lake of fire and sulphur where the beast and the false prophet were, and they* (i.e. the devil and the beast and the false prophet) *will be tormented day and night for ever and ever.'* That is how these verses are punctuated in the Authorized Version, which in this case is correct. The devil, the beast and the false prophet will be perpetually tormented, but the human supporters of the antichrist will be destroyed.

However there is a second more serious problem in verse 10. If the devil, the beast and the false prophet are to be tormented continuously for ever that can only mean that they will exist for ever. Yet the letter to the Hebrews tells us that Jesus took on our human nature, '...*that through death he might destroy him who has the power of death, that is, the devil.*' (Hebrews 2.14) Similarly Paul wrote in 1 Corinthians 15.24 that when Jesus delivers the kingdom to God the Father at the end, it will be '...*after destroying every rule and every authority and power,*' by which he meant the devil and all his angels. So whether Jesus is going to destroy the devil or destroy the devil and all his angels, the devil cannot continue to live for ever as Revelation 20.10 suggests. Moreover Paul said in 2 Thessalonians 2.8 that the beast will be destroyed too. '...*the Lord Jesus will slay him with the breath of his mouth and destroy him by his appearing and his coming,*' he wrote. The Lord will kill him and destroy every vestige of him. So how can Revelation 20.10 be true when it implies that the devil, the beast and the false prophet will live for ever?

Some people suggest that the Greek phrase *eis tous aiōnas tōn aiōnōn*, translated 'for ever and ever', could mean 'until the perfect age comes', when the torment of the devil and his collaborators would cease. The Greek word *eis* occurs hundreds of times in the New Testament but

136

only in three verses[69] does it unambiguously mean 'until', and these are not in the phrase *eis tous aiōnas tōn aiōnōn*. The phrase *eis tous aiōnas tōn aiōnōn* occurs eleven times in the New Testament referring to God's eternity, where it can mean nothing other than 'for ever'. For example '...*our God and Father; to whom be the glory for ever and ever*' (Galatians 1.4,5); "...*I died, and behold I am alive for evermore*" (Revelation 1.18); '...*to him who is seated on the throne, who lives for ever and ever*' (Revelation 4.9); '... *God who lives for ever and ever*' (Revelation 15.7). In such verses the phrase couldn't possibly mean merely 'until the perfect age comes'; it can only mean 'for ever'. That's how New Testament Greek says 'for ever'. So when we come to the only two other instances of the phrase in the Bible, one referring to smoke going up (Revelation 14.11) and the other referring to the torment of the devil, the beast and the false prophet (Revelation 20.10), it can only mean what it means everywhere else in the Bible: 'for ever and ever'.

As we saw earlier, the phrase 'the smoke of their torment goes up for ever and ever' is not intended in the Bible to be taken literally, except perhaps in the sense that the memory of it will endure for ever. So when Revelation 20.10 says that the devil, the beast and the false prophet will be tormented day and night for ever and ever, is that intended to be understood literally or not?

John Wesley adopted two principles in interpreting the Bible. (i) '*It is a stated rule in interpreting scripture never to depart from the plain, literal sense, unless it implies an absurdity,*' and (ii) '*The general rule of interpreting scripture*

---

[69] The three New Testament verses where *eis* means 'until' are Acts 25.21, 1 Thessalonians 4.15 and 2 Timothy 1.12.

is this: the literal sense of every text is to be taken, if it be not contrary to some other texts. But in that case, the obscure text is to be interpreted by those which speak more plainly.[70] He mentioned both principles together in his sermon 'A Call to Backsliders': *'It does not appear that we have any reason to depart from the literal meaning* [of Hebrews 6.4] *as it neither implies any absurdity, nor contradicts any other scriptures.'*[71]

If Revelation 20.10 were interpreted literally it would clearly contradict many other scriptures. So how else could it be interpreted? Jesus's teaching gives us a clue. In order to highlight the importance of something that he was teaching, Jesus would sometimes express it in exaggerated terms. For example:

- *"It is easier for a camel to go through the eye of a needle than for a rich man to enter the kingdom of God."* (Mark 10.25) If he meant that literally then no rich man would be able to enter God's kingdom, and that would have excluded Abraham for a start.

- *"If your right eye causes you to sin, pluck it out and throw it away... And if your right hand causes you to sin, cut it off and throw it away; it is better that you lose one of your members than that your whole body go into hell* (Gehenna).*"* (Matthew 5.29,30) If Jesus meant that literally, then most of his disciples would have been physically disabled.[72]

---

[70] From a letter written by Wesley to Samuel Furly.

[71] *A Call to Backsliders.* Sermon 86, I (4), 1778.

[72] I find it interesting that some Christians insist on taking literally the words about going to hell (actually the rubbish tip) but they never take literally the first part of the same sentence that says they should cut off their hand if it causes them to sin. It is intellectually

- *"…he who eats my flesh and drinks my blood has eternal life…"* (John 6.54) He hardly intended that literally!

- *"But now… let him who has no sword sell his mantle and buy one."* (Luke 22.36) On the way to his arrest Jesus warned his disciples of trouble ahead for them too. But when they replied that they did have two swords he immediately told them that two were quite sufficient: he hadn't literally meant them all to sell their precious coats and start killing people.

Paul could also exaggerate at times. '*…continue in the faith, stable and steadfast, not shifting from the hope of the gospel which you heard, which has been preached to every creature under heaven…*' (Colossians 1.23, literally 'which has been proclaimed in all creation under heaven'.) When Paul wrote this around AD 61 he had not even reached Spain, and there is no evidence whatsoever that the gospel had been preached to every single inhabitant of Africa, Asia and America as well as to every animal, bird, fish and insect!

I'm not going to suggest that the devil and his two collaborators will avoid torment altogether. If people who have engaged in genocide, torture and crimes against humanity will be punished in proportion to the suffering they have caused, then the antichrist and the false prophet will certainly be among them. And if wicked people will

---

dishonest to dismiss as figurative the words one doesn't want to believe and to insist on taking literally the words that for some reason one does want to believe. If Jesus meant the first part of the sentence figuratively is it so unreasonable to suggest that he meant the second part figuratively too?

suffer, how much greater must be the torment that Satan and his demonic servants will have to suffer! That is why the demons asked Jesus, *"Have you come here to torment us before the time?"* (Matthew 8.29) But again, this period of divine retribution will not last for ever, for Jesus came to destroy the devil, and since the last enemy to be destroyed is death, once death has been thrown into the lake of fire only those whose names are written in the book of life will remain. (Hebrews 2.14; 1 Corinthians 15.26; Revelation 20.14,15)

Therefore, if the Lord Jesus and his apostle Paul could use exaggerated language, never intending it to be taken literally, why shouldn't John have done the same when he wrote that those three characters would be tormented for ever? John's passionate motivation in writing Revelation was to encourage believers in Christ to stand firm in their loyalty to Jesus even if it cost them their lives. It is likely that he wrote Revelation at a time when it was widely believed that Nero, the cruellest Roman emperor of all, was going to return from the dead and rule once again in the form of the antichrist.[73] John was desperately concerned that if those who had come to believe in Christ surrendered to the antichrist, they would lose their wonderful inheritance of eternal life in God's kingdom. He encouraged them to stand fast against the antichrist's demand for worship by reminding them in Revelation 14.9-11 of their fate if they gave in; and by assuring them in Revelation 20.10 that eventually the antichrist, the false prophet and even the devil would suffer the worst kind of fate possible. John wanted to provide them

---

[73] *The Revelation of John, Volume 2*. W.Barclay, The Daily Study Bible, Revised Edition, The Saint Andrew Press, 1976. Commentary on Revelation chapter 13.

with a strong encouragement to stand firm in their newly found commitment to the true Christ. '*Here is a call for the endurance of the saints, those who keep the commandments of God and the faith of Jesus,*' he wrote. (Revelation 14.12) John deliberately used exaggerated language to emphasize the seriousness of his message, language that he did not seriously intend or expect anyone to take literally.

Summary

People who believe in Jesus, who put their trust in him as saviour and live with him as their Lord, will not be among those present at the last judgement. They already have the promise of eternal life, and will be raised to everlasting life on the day of resurrection. Jesus said, *"I am the resurrection and the life; he who believes in me, though he die, yet shall he live, and whoever lives and believes in me shall never die."* (John 11.25,26)

Those who die not believing in Jesus as saviour and Lord will be judged by their behaviour in the light of what they have known of God's will.

(i)   Death When they die their spirits enter Hades, the realm of the departed, in a state akin to sleep, to await the day of judgement.

(ii) Judgement At the end of Christ's initial thousand-year reign over this present earth they will be resurrected, i.e. returned to a state of full consciousness in bodily form. In the presence of Jesus as judge they will then learn whether or not they are to be granted eternal life in God's kingdom.

(iii) <u>Salvation</u> Those who have not knowingly rejected Jesus as saviour, who have not lived manifestly wicked lives and died unrepentant, who have been kind to people in trouble, who have earnestly tried to live as good a life as best they know how, and who have been grateful to God for giving them life insofar as they have known him, will be granted eternal life in his kingdom. They will initially join resurrected believers in heaven while God creates a new earth to be their final dwelling place.

(iv) <u>Damnation</u> If they are not granted eternal life they will all experience extreme remorse. Some at least will then suffer some kind of painful retribution in proportion to whatever suffering they have caused on earth, for God is a God of justice, and he has promised to avenge wrong-doing, particularly the murder of his servants. (Romans 12.19; Deuteronomy 32.43; Revelation 19.2) Finally their life will be terminated for ever in what Revelation calls 'the second death', along with the devil and his angels.

The Bible does not teach that the destiny of the damned is to spend eternity being tormented in hell. Their destiny is annihilation. If the penalty of sin is to be everlasting torment then Jesus Christ did not suffer the penalty of sin in our place.

Most of us spend a lot of money insuring against events that will probably never happen. How much more sensible it is to insure against an event which most definitely will happen – the day of judgement. The one sure way to avoid standing before Jesus as judge on that day is to put your life now into his hands as saviour. *"…he who hears my word and believes him who sent me, has eternal life; he does not come into judgement, but has passed from death to life."* (John 5.24) *"…therefore choose life, that you… may live!"* (Deuteronomy 30.19)

10

The Destiny Of
The Saved

A big question

This chapter answers the question, "If we believe in Jesus, shall we spend eternity on earth or in heaven?"

For many Christians the answer is obvious: it will be in heaven. That's certainly the answer given by many traditional hymns. Before my sisters and I went to sleep our mother used to sing a hymn that ended: *'Take me when I die to heaven, happy there with thee to dwell'*. Similarly the Christmas carol 'Once in Royal David's City', which starts off every Christmas Eve carol service at King's College, Cambridge, ends with the words:

> *Not in that poor lowly stable with the oxen standing by*
> *We shall see him, but in heaven set at God's right hand on high,*
> *When like stars his children crowned, all in white shall wait around.*

Cecil Frances Alexander

The trouble is that if I had to wait around for ever, even with a crown on my head, I'd die of boredom. And for the average non-believer who doesn't particularly desire to see Jesus anyway, telling him that he can have eternal life in heaven in the presence of Jesus and his angels is simply a turn-off. In fact I am sure that the rather nebulous image of eternal life that most Christians have is a principal reason that we don't share the gospel more enthusiastically. How can we hope to excite anyone about something if, to be honest, it doesn't excite us very much?

I was once at a church luncheon club where an elderly man was complaining that his body was wearing out.

"Never mind," I said. "If you trust in Jesus you can live for ever."

"I don't want to live for ever," he replied.

Strangely enough the Bible itself doesn't seem to agree with traditional church teaching on this subject. Almost without exception it teaches that the eternal destiny of believers will not be in heaven but on earth, on earth with the resurrected Lord Jesus Christ. For example, we are to pray that God's kingdom will come *on earth*. (Matthew 6.10) The Lord will become king over all *the earth*. (Zechariah 14.9) The saints from all nations will reign *on earth*, Revelation tells us. In a vision of heaven John heard angelic beings worshipping Jesus with this song:

> *"Worthy art thou to take the scroll and to open*
> *its seals, for thou wast slain and by thy blood*
> *didst ransom men for God from every tribe*
> *and tongue and people and nation,*

> *and hast made them a kingdom and priests to*
> *our God, and they shall reign <u>on earth</u>."*
> (Revelation 5.9,10)

So do such scriptures describe in some symbolical way how things are now, or are they a literal description of how things will be in the life to come? Let's have a closer look at what the Bible teaches about God's plans for our future.

The kingdom of God

In John's gospel the good news is mainly about eternal life, but in the other three gospels and to some extent in the book of Acts the good news is all about the kingdom of God:

- <u>Matthew</u> *'And Jesus went about all the cities and villages, teaching in their synagogues and preaching the gospel* (good news) *of the kingdom...'* (Matthew 9.35)
- <u>Mark</u> '*...Jesus came into Galilee, preaching the gospel of God, and saying, "The time is fulfilled, and the kingdom of God is at hand..."*' (Mark 1.14,15)
- <u>Luke</u> *'When you pray, say... "Thy kingdom come."'* (Luke 11,2)
- <u>Acts</u> To his apostles, Jesus '*...presented himself alive after his passion by many proofs, appearing to them during forty days, and speaking of the kingdom of God.'* (Acts 1.3)

Jesus based all his teaching on the Old Testament, which he said he had come to fulfil. *"Think not that I have come to abolish the law and the prophets; I have come not to abolish them but to fulfil them."* (Matthew 5.17) All his audience were Jews, and they would have understood from the Old Testament what he meant by the kingdom of God. The Old Testament taught that God would send a king, a descendant of King David, who would rule the earth with justice for ever on the throne of his famous ancestor.

> *There shall come forth a shoot from the stump of Jesse* (King David's father), *and a branch shall grow out of his roots. And the Spirit of the Lord shall rest upon him, the spirit of wisdom and understanding, the spirit of counsel and might, the spirit of knowledge and the fear of the Lord. …with righteousness he shall judge the poor, and decide with equity for the meek of the earth; and he shall smite the earth with the rod of his mouth, and with the breath of his lips he shall slay the wicked.* (Isaiah 11.1-4)

> *For to us a child is born, to us a son is given; and the government will be upon his shoulder, and his name will be called "Wonderful Counsellor, Mighty God, Everlasting Father, Prince of Peace." Of the increase of his government and of peace there will be no end, upon the throne of David, and over his kingdom, to establish it, and to uphold it with justice and with righteousness from this time forth and for evermore.* (Isaiah 9.6,7)

> *But you, O Bethlehem Ephrathah, who are little to be among the clans of Judah, from you shall come forth for me one who is to be ruler in Israel, whose origin is from of old, from ancient days. ...he shall be great to the ends of the earth.* (Micah 5.2,4)

The prophets realized that if the coming descendant of King David was to reign for ever over the earth he would have to be more than human. His origin would be 'from ancient days' (a description normally reserved for God – see Daniel 7.9); he would have to be an 'everlasting Father' (again, a description previously applied only to God – see Deuteronomy 33.27 and Malachi 2.10); in fact he would somehow have to be the 'Mighty God' himself! Obviously these were all prophecies of Jesus, who was both the Son of Man and the Son of God. But what's important here is that they all foretold that Jesus's everlasting reign would be *on the earth*. And Jesus said that he had come to fulfil all that the prophets had foretold.

A new earth

The old Jewish prophets had two dilemmas. First, if the coming king was to rule for ever he would have to be more than human. Second, if he was to rule over the earth for ever, then something serious had to happen to the earth. For they were realistic about the present earth's condition: it could not last for ever. '*Of old thou didst lay the foundation of the earth, and the heavens are the work of thy hands. They will perish, but thou dost endure; they will all wear out like a garment.*' (Psalm 102.25,26) "*…the heavens will vanish like smoke, the earth will wear out like a garment…*" (Isaiah 51.6)

We can see the earth wearing out right now, in the alarming loss of topsoil and the increasing desertification of once fertile lands; the disappearance of tropical rainforests and vital sources of fresh water like Lake Chad in western Africa; the pollution of the air, oceans and outer space by industrial waste products and human garbage; the fast diminishing natural resources of oil, gas, copper, rare earths and other elements that are vital to contemporary life; and the continuing loss of species in the animal, plant and other kingdoms.

However, the Lord told the prophets not to worry. Just as he had made this earth long ago so he planned to make a new one, even better than the one we have now. "*…the earth will wear out like a garment, and they who dwell in it will die like gnats; but my salvation will be for ever, and my deliverance will never be ended.*" (Isaiah 51.6) "*For behold, I create new heavens and a new earth.*" (Isaiah 65.17) In the New Testament Peter wrote, '*…according to his promise we wait for new heavens and a new earth in which righteousness dwells.*' (2 Peter 3.13) And John was given a vision of this new earth: '*Then I saw a new heaven and a new earth; for the first heaven and the first earth had passed away, and the sea was no more.*' (Revelation 21.1) The Bible consistently tells us that God is going to make another planet Earth.

The present earth has acquired many defects since God first made it, when it was 'very good'. (Genesis 1.31) Thorns and thistles have appeared. Mountains have risen up resulting in earthquakes, volcanic eruptions and avalanches; oceans have spread out producing storms, floods and tsunamis.

Some regions have become too hot or dry for comfort, while others are too cold or wet; animals and plants suffer from diseases and compete against each other for survival; too much sun causes skin cancer and too little produces vitamin D deficiency. But God has promised to put everything right by starting again, and this time the earth he creates will not be spoilt as a result of mankind's sin.

> *The wilderness and the dry land shall be glad, the desert shall rejoice and blossom…* (Isaiah 35.1)

> *Instead of the thorn shall come up the cypress; instead of the brier shall come up the myrtle…* (Isaiah 55.13)

> *The wolf shall dwell with the lamb, and the leopard shall lie down with the kid, and the calf and the lion and the fatling for ever, and a little child shall lead them… They shall not hurt or destroy in all my holy mountain; for the earth shall be full of the knowledge of the Lord as the waters cover the sea.* (Isaiah 11.6,9)

> *There shall no more be anything accursed…* (Revelation 22.3)

> *"Then I saw a new heaven and a new earth, for the first heaven and the earth had passed away… God himself will be with them; he will wipe away every tear from their eyes,*

> *and death shall be no more, neither shall*
> *there be mourning nor crying nor pain any*
> *more, for the former things have passed away."*
> (Revelation 21.1,4)

In the Authorized Version's literal translation of Matthew 19.28 Jesus tells his disciples, *"Verily, I say unto you, that ye which have followed me, in the regeneration when the Son of man shall sit in the throne of his glory, ye also shall sit upon twelve thrones, judging the twelve tribes of Israel."* According to my vast Greek-English lexicon[74] the Greek word *paliggenesia*, which is translated as 'regeneration', means *'recreation, or the restoration of a thing to its pristine state.'* Again, in the Authorized Version of Acts 3.21 Peter declares that heaven must receive Jesus *'...until the times of restitution of all things, which God hath spoken by the mouth of all his holy prophets since the world began.'* According to the lexicon the words translated as the 'restitution of all things' mean *'the restoration not only of the true theocracy* (rule by God) *but also of the more perfect state of even physical things which existed before the fall.'*

Thus the Bible unambiguously declares that the new earth which God will make will be just like the present earth was before Adam and Eve fell into sin. Thorns and thistles will no longer be the bane of gardeners and farmers. All the species of animals and plants that perished in the flood or have disappeared in more recent years will be restored. Woolly mammoths, dinosaurs of all kinds and even the

---

[74] *A Greek-English lexicon of the New Testament.* Grimm's Wilke's Clavis Novi Testamenti, translated, revised and enlarged by Joseph H. Thayer, fourth edition, T & T Clark, Edinburgh, 1901.

duck-billed platypus will be back! But the wildest animals will be so tame and friendly that even a child would safely be able to hitch a lift on a velociraptor!

People will inhabit the new earth

If God is going to take the trouble of making a brand new earth fit for human beings it's obvious that human beings are going to live in it. Otherwise what would be the point of making it? Since death will be no more, those who live in it will not die. And if they are not going to die they will have to be people who have been granted eternal life, either through their faith in Christ while they were alive, or else at the last judgement in response to how they lived without any knowledge of him. In other words, only the saved will inhabit the new earth. And that is pretty well what the Bible says: '*Outside are the dogs and sorcerers and fornicators and murderers and idolaters, and every one who loves and practises falsehood.*' (Revelation 22.15)

The saved will have been resurrected from death in physical bodies that no longer have any defects. '*Then the eyes of the blind shall be opened, and the ears of the deaf unstopped; then shall the lame man leap like a hart, and the tongue of the dumb sing for joy.*' (Isaiah 35.5,6) When Jesus healed the blind, deaf, dumb and lame he was giving people a foretaste of his kingdom to come, when no one will be disabled or sick.

These resurrected bodies will be real bodies, just like Jesus Christ's resurrection body. '*...the Lord Jesus Christ, who will change our lowly body to be like his glorious body...*' (Philippians 3.20,21) On the evening that Jesus rose from the dead he told his astonished disciples, *"...a spirit has not flesh and bones as you see that I have."* (Luke 24.39) In his resurrection body Jesus ate fish and bread; he looked forward to eating another Passover meal when he returned; and he looked forward to drinking some fresh ('new') grape juice with them. (Luke 24.42; John 21.9,15; Luke 22.14-18) People won't need physical food or drink in heaven, which is why Jesus said that he wouldn't eat a Passover or drink again of the fruit of the vine until he came back to the earth in his resurrection body to establish his kingdom. And it's a resurrection body like his body that we shall have if we believe in him. We shall have a body that's designed to eat earthly food and drink earthly drink, in other words *a body designed to live on the earth.*

'*The heavens are the Lord's heavens, but the earth he has given to the sons of men.*' (Psalm 115.16)

In fact the Bible clearly states that everyone who is saved through faith in Christ and is granted a place in his kingdom will live on the wonderful new earth that God has promised.

- The meek will live on the earth. (Matthew 5.5)
- Jesus's original apostles and the saved people of Israel will live on the recreated earth. (Matthew 19.28)
- People from every people group, language and nation who have been saved by the blood of Christ will live on the earth. (Revelation 5.9,10)

So we shall not go up to the heavenly city: instead the heavenly city will come down to us. We shall not dwell for ever with God: instead he will dwell for ever with us, in the person of Jesus Christ the king. *'And I saw the holy city, new Jerusalem, coming down out of heaven from God, prepared as a bride adorned for her husband; and I heard a loud voice from the throne saying, "Behold, the dwelling of God is with men. He will dwell with them, and they shall be his people, and God himself will be with them."'* (Revelation 21.2,3)

But doesn't the Bible say. . .?

Nevertheless, some Christians believe that Paul's letter to the Ephesians tells a different story. Ephesians 1.20 says that Christ is currently seated at the right hand of God in heavenly places. Ephesians 2.4-7 then says:

> *…God, who is rich in mercy, out of the great love with which he loved us, even when we were dead through our trespasses, made us alive together with Christ (by grace you have been saved), and raised us up with him, and made us sit with him in the heavenly places in Christ Jesus, that in the coming ages he might show the immeasurable riches of his grace in kindness toward us in Christ Jesus.*

These verses are interpreted by some people to mean that the saved will spend the coming ages seated with Christ in heavenly places rather than earthly ones. Some who hold this view also teach that the Bible verses referring to a future life on the earth refer only to Jewish believers and perhaps also to some of the first Gentile believers to whom Paul wrote in his earlier letters. I've discussed the latter teaching in Annex 2.

For a start Paul doesn't say that God *will* raise us up with Christ and seat us with him in heavenly places: he says that God has done this already. In Ephesians 2.1,2 he wrote, '*And you he made alive, when you were dead through the trespasses and sins in which you once walked...*' That was about something that God had already done for the believers in Ephesus. So in verses 4 to 6 Paul reiterated what God had done for them and then he expanded it: '*God... made us alive together with Christ... and raised us up with him, and made us sit with him in the heavenly places...*'

Paul was saying that believers in Christ are spiritually alive right now and are seated with Christ in heavenly places right now. I understand this to mean that right now we can share in Christ's authority and victory over the evil one. *"All authority in heaven and on earth has been given to me."* (Matthew 28.18) *"...I have given you authority to tread upon serpents and scorpions, <u>and over all the power of the enemy</u>..."* (Luke 10.19) '*...we are not contending against flesh and blood, but against... the spiritual hosts of wickedness <u>in the heavenly places</u>.*' (Ephesians 6.12) We have to be seated with Christ now in the heavenly places by faith, in order to fight and defeat the evil one who also inhabits heavenly places.

Then Paul went on to state what God *would* do in the coming ages. Having spoken about the amazing privileges God had granted to believers in this age: he went on to tell them that in the coming ages God would treat them with absolutely immeasurable grace and kindness.

When Jesus is king. . .

Please excuse me now for repeating a passage I wrote in *Z: The Final Generation.*

> *Try to imagine life in a world in which everyone lives in perfect accordance with God's will. A world in which everyone loves his neighbour as himself, in which everyone is kind and helpful and generous and cheerful and truthful and responsible and trustworthy. A world in which nobody is selfish or greedy or dishonest. In such a world no one will starve, no one will be homeless, no one will be lonely, no one will be afraid. There will be no war, no terrorism, no robbery, no violence. There will be no need for armies, police, judges or prisons, all of which consume labour and material resources and leave society poorer. People will never have to lock their doors or windows or cars or bicycles. In the business world there will no longer be vast and morally unjustifiable differences in the pay of owners and employees; disputes will be resolved amicably and fairly without any need for strikes, and no one will have to work excessive hours in a stressful environment. With no disease and no physical or mental handicaps there will be no need for an expensive health service. Everyone will have everything they need!*

That's how it's going to be in the world to come!

...nation shall not lift up sword against nation, neither shall they learn war any more; but they shall sit every man under his vine and under his fig tree, and none shall make them afraid; for the mouth of the Lord of hosts has spoken. (Micah 4.3-4)

Then justice will dwell in the wilderness, and righteousness abide in the fruitful field. And the effect of righteousness will be peace, and the result of righteousness, quietness and trust for ever. (Isaiah 32.16,17)

"...all these blessings shall come upon you and overtake you, if you obey the voice of the Lord your God. Blessed shall you be in the city, and blessed shall you be in the field. Blessed shall be the fruit of your body, and the fruit of your ground, and the fruit of your beasts, the increase of your cattle, and the young of your flock. Blessed shall be your basket and your kneading-trough." (Deuteronomy 28.2-5)

And the ransomed of the Lord shall return, and come to Zion with singing; everlasting joy shall be upon their heads; they shall obtain joy and gladness, and sorrow and sighing shall flee away. (Isaiah 51.11)

11

A New Heaven Or New Heavens?

All things new

In Revelation chapter 21 verse 1 we read, '*Then I saw a new heaven and a new earth*,' and in verse 5 we read, '*...He who sat upon the throne said, "Behold, I make all things new."*'

- The word 'heaven' could mean either everything apart from the earth, or just the earth's atmosphere. (Jesus spoke about the birds of the air in various places, and the word used for 'air' is exactly the same word used for 'heaven' in Revelation 21.1.)
- The Greek word translated 'new' can mean 'brand new', 'new and better', or even 'of a new unprecedented kind'.
- Presumably 'all things' doesn't include God himself, the holy angels, people who will have already been made new through resurrection to eternal life, nor those who will be condemned to final death.

'Behold, I make all things new' could mean one of three possibilities:

(i) God is going to replace everything with something totally different. There will be a new earth and its atmosphere, but no sun, moon or stars, and no day and night.

(ii) God is going to remake everything, apart from the items listed above that he will not replace. There will be a new and better earth, a new sun and moon, new planets and stars, and perhaps even new space and time.

(iii) God is going to renew only those things in the natural world that have been corrupted as a result of sin, i.e. the earth, its atmosphere and the world of nature, but nothing more.

(i) God will replace everything with something totally different

This is the most extreme possibility. There will be neither sun nor moon nor (presumably) planets and stars in the age to come, but just a new earth. Revelation 21.23-25 says, *'And the city has no need of sun or moon to shine upon it, for the glory of God is its light, and its lamp is the Lamb. ...there shall be no night there...'* Similarly Revelation 22.5 says, *'And night shall be no more; they need no light of lamp or sun, for the Lord God will be their light...'*

If there is to be no sun, moon or night, the world will be totally different from how it is now. Isaiah 60.19,20 seems to support this idea. *'The sun shall be no more your light by day, nor for brightness shall the moon give light to you by night; but the Lord will be your everlasting light, and your God will be your glory. Your sun shall no more go down, nor your moon withdraw itself; for the Lord will be your everlasting light, and your days of mourning shall be ended.'* It looks very much as though John was quoting from these two verses.

In further support of the idea that there will be no night, Zechariah 14.5-7 says, *'Then the Lord your God will come, and all the holy ones with him. On that day... there shall be continuous day (it is known to the Lord), not day and not night, for at evening time there shall be light.'*

The problem is that all this seems to contradict many other verses in scripture. For example Isaiah 66.22,23 says, *"For as the new heavens and the new earth which I will make shall remain before me, says that Lord; so shall your descendants and your name remain. From new moon to new moon, and from sabbath to sabbath, all flesh shall come to worship before me, says the Lord."* Isaiah foresaw the continuing existence of a moon, as well as of a sun, because in those days the months were set by the moon and the hours of the Sabbath were set by sunrise and sunset. And if there is to be sunrise and sunset then there will also be day and night.

There will still be seasons, for the passage in Zechariah 14.8 goes on to say, *'On that day living waters shall flow out from Jerusalem... it shall continue in summer as in winter,'* and Revelation 22.2 speaks of twelve months in a year, even in the heavenly city. Furthermore Isaiah says that when God creates new heavens and a new earth people will *'...plant vineyards and eat their fruit'* (Isaiah 65.17,21), and Micah says that *'...they shall sit every man under his vine and under his fig tree...'* (Micah 4.4) It is hard to envisage summer and winter months and natural growing seasons unless the earth continues to orbit the sun on an inclined axis. And if it orbits the sun it must also rotate, otherwise one face will be too hot to support life and the other face too cold. And if it rotates there will still be days and nights. Finally, without days and nights there cannot be weeks, and without weeks there cannot be a weekly Sabbath. Yet God said that the observance of the Sabbath every week was to be a perpetual covenant for ever. (Exodus 31.16,17) We are back to life more or less as we know it.

So what is the explanation of the verses in Isaiah and Revelation chapter 21 that suggest there won't be any sun or moon? Well, they do not specifically say this. They say that the presence of the Lord will bring so much light that the light of the sun and moon will not be *needed*. And in Revelation this light is said to be in the holy city, not throughout the earth. So it is the people in the city who will have no need of sun or moon and who will not experience darkness at night, not the earth as a whole.

When Zechariah prophesied, '*On that day... there shall be continuous day (it is known to the Lord), not day and not night,*' he was most likely referring to the actual 24-hour day of Christ's return. Just as God halted the earth's rotation for about a day to give Joshua time to completely defeat the Amorites (Joshua 10.12-14) so he might delay the onset of night on the day that Jesus returns to give him time to defeat the armies of the antichrist in the battle of Armageddon.

The only reason I can think of to support the idea that God will replace everything with something totally different is that natural stars, including the sun, could not last for eternity. No doubt the final answer lies in one of the many future ages yet to come, which even the Bible does not describe. A lot can happen in our first 5 billion years!

(ii) God will remake everything that currently exists

When the Bible writers looked up into the sky at night they didn't see space as we know it to be. They knew what God had told them, but they were not omniscient. So to their eyes the heavens looked like a kind of canopy stretched out over the earth.[75] Genesis Chapter 1 says that the sun, moon and stars and birds all occupy 'the firmament of the heavens'. So it must have seemed obvious to the writers of the Bible that if a bird could fall out of the firmament then in theory the stars could also. Hence when Isaiah wrote, *'All the host of heaven shall rot away, and the skies roll up like a scroll. All their host shall fall, as leaves fall from the vine, like leaves falling from the fig tree'* (Isaiah 34.4), he was picturing the sun, moon and stars falling out of the sky above us and landing on the ground. Of course, such a passage might be interpreted as poetic or symbolical language, but when the same prophet reported God's words, *"For behold, I create new heavens and a new earth,"* (Isaiah 65.17) he would almost certainly have understood this to include the sun, moon and stars, because these were an essential part of the heavens. The writers of the Bible would have found it very difficult to conceive how God might recreate the earth and sky without recreating everything in them at the same time, including the sun, moon and stars.

Similarly, when John saw a new heaven and earth in Revelation 21.1 and God said in Revelation 21.5, *"Behold,*

---

[75] Psalm 104.2 says that God has *'stretched out the heavens like a tent,'* and Isaiah 40.22 says that God *'stretches out the heavens like a curtain, and spreads them like a tent to dwell in.'*

I make all things new," John would almost certainly have understood 'all things' to include the sun, the moon and all the stars. So there will still be a sun, moon and stars, but they will be new ones.

One reason God might want to make *everything* new is because somehow it has all been corrupted through sin. Although everything was 'very good' when God first made it (Genesis 1.31) Job said, *"The stars are not pure in* [God's] *sight"*. (Job 25.5 AV) If that is literally true it suggests that the stars too may have to be remade.

(iii) God will renew only the earth and its atmosphere

Nevertheless there are many other reasons for believing that it will be only the earth and its atmosphere that God is going to recreate.

In his letter to the Romans Paul wrote, '...*the creation waits with eager longing for the revealing of the sons of God; for the creation was subjected to futility, not of its own will but by the will of him who subjected it in hope; because the creation itself will be set free from its bondage to decay and obtain the glorious liberty of the children of God. We know that the whole creation has been groaning in travail together until now; and not only the creation, but we ourselves... as we wait for... the redemption of our bodies.'* (Romans 8.19-23)

- The word translated 'futility' can mean 'weakness'. In the world of nature it corresponds to the weakness in our physical bodies, which will be 'sown in weakness and raised in power'. (1 Corinthians 15.43)

- The word translated 'decay' generally means 'perishing'. In the world of nature it corresponds to our perishable physical bodies, which will be 'sown perishable but raised imperishable'. (1 Corinthians 15.42)

In these verses Paul was thinking about the consequences of Adam's sin in the natural world. Just as decay and death entered human bodies as a result of sin, so the world of nature was altered, not only by the introduction of thorns and thistles, but by disease, degeneration and death. Even without the help of humans, species have continually been dying out. So by 'the whole creation' Paul almost certainly meant the living but perishing world of nature, not the entire universe. The Living Bible translation makes this clear: *'For on that day thorns and thistles, sin, death and decay... will all disappear, and the world around us will share in the glorious freedom from sin which God's children enjoy. For we know that even the things of nature, like animals and plants, suffer in sickness and death as they await this great event.'* (Romans 8.20-22 TLB)

In this passage Paul was not assigning any idea of moral decay to the world of nature, only physical decay. And apart from a literal reading of the words in Job about the stars not being pure there is no suggestion in the Bible that God cursed the sun or the moon or anything as a result of man's sin except life on earth (Genesis 3.17,18), and the physical changes to the earth that took place as a result of the Flood.

Therefore it is only the earth and its atmosphere that needs to be replaced.

2 Peter 3.6,7 draws a close analogy between the forthcoming destruction of the earth by fire and the previous destruction of the earth by a flood. '*...the world that then existed was deluged with water and perished. But by the same word the heavens and earth that now exist have been stored up for fire, being kept until the day of judgement and destruction of ungodly men.*' When Peter wrote 'the world that then existed' he was referring only to the earth and its atmosphere. So when he went on to say that by the same word the present heavens and earth will be destroyed by fire he was almost certainly referring only to the earth and its atmosphere. Peter connected both events with the destruction of the ungodly, so in both cases it is only the earth where the ungodly have lived that needs to be destroyed. Since the planet cannot be totally destroyed by fire without destroying its atmosphere at the same time, that too will have to be replaced.

In Psalm 89.35-37 the Lord made a promise so serious that he backed it up by swearing, even though Jesus said we should never swear! Here's what he said. *"Once for all I have sworn by my holiness; I will not lie to David. His line shall endure for ever, his throne as long as the sun before me. Like the moon it shall be established for ever; it shall stand firm while the skies endure."* The Lord would never have used those words in a most solemn oath if he knew that one day he was going to destroy the present sun, moon and skies.

Psalm 119.89 says, '*For ever, O Lord, thy word is firmly fixed in the heavens.*' The Bible tells us that God named the stars. (Psalm 147.4) There is philological evidence[76] that the oldest names for the stars and their constellations (not always the current ones) spelt out in every language the story of creation and redemption from start to finish. (E.g. Virgo the Virgin Mary, Leo the Lion of Judah, Libra the scales of God's judgement, etc.) That is why Psalm 19.1-4 says, '*The heavens are telling the glory of God; and the firmament proclaims his handiwork... There is no speech, nor are there words; their voice is not heard; yet their voice goes out through all the earth, and their words to the end of the world.*' If God has fixed his word *for ever* in the existing stars and constellations he will hardly destroy them all and remake them again in exactly the same positions as before.

So I believe that God will not remake the stars, sun or moon, and that they will continue to exist as they are. I am supported in this by Professor J. Richard Middleton. In his scholarly work, *A New Heaven and a New Earth*, published by Baker Publishing Group in December 2014, he concludes that God will remake only the earth and its atmosphere.

---

[76] See *The Heavens Declare* by W.D.Banks, Impact Books Inc., Family Reading Centre, Kent, UK, ISBN 0-089228-101-4; and *The Witness of the Stars* by E.W.Bullinger, reprinted by Kregel Publications, Grand Rapids, Michigan, ISBN 0-8254-2245-0.

Epilogue

The Bible's True After All – So What?

Making a difference

Some things you learn make little or no difference to your life. The weather forecaster announces, "There will be snow on the Scottish hills today." Unless you're a Scottish shepherd or you're there for a skiing holiday that weather forecast probably won't affect you in the slightest.

"The average life expectancy is now 82 years." That's certainly good news, but knowing you might live a year or two longer than you thought isn't going to make very much difference right now, unless you are nearly 80!

But what about, "We have confirmed our initial diagnosis of your condition. I'm very sorry to tell you that you probably have three more months to live at the most."

Now that *would* make a difference. If you still had the strength you might want spend your remaining time doing some of the things you'd always wanted to do but never got round to doing or never dared to try. Perhaps you'd visit Israel or Tahiti, or take a Mediterranean cruise, or do a skydive, or fulfil a lifelong fantasy and book a fortnight's holiday in a naturist resort. You'd want to get your affairs in order for your family; make a will if necessary; write down your wishes for your funeral. You might want to seek reconciliation with someone you'd fallen out with; forgive someone who had wronged you; or even ask forgiveness from someone whom you had wronged. You might simply want to tell someone something that you'd always wanted to say but somehow never got round to.

Your priorities would change dramatically. Some things that had previously seemed important to you – perhaps the possibility of promotion at work or the value of your savings or shares – would suddenly become totally irrelevant. On the other hand a question that had never seriously crossed your mind might suddenly become the most important question of all. And that question might be, "If some people really will continue to live after they die in a real kind of life that fulfils all their deepest desires, what must I do to join them?"

The ultimate good news

If the Bible is true after all then the news it tells us is the most exciting, awe-inspiring, life-changing news that anyone could ever learn or hear. The Bible tells us that this short life on earth is intended to be only a taster, not the main course. The main course is available to anyone who will trust one hundred per cent in Jesus Christ and his promises. For the special offer announced in the Bible is far more than the news that there is a God who loves you, who is willing to forgive your sins if you repent of them, and who wants to have a personal relationship with you now and for ever. It is more than a promise to rescue you from everything that enslaves you and to give you instead a new life filled with hope and joy and fulfilment. It is all that, it really is, yet it is far, far more than that. As Saint Paul wrote, '*If for this life only we have hoped in Christ, we are of all men most to be pitied.*' (1 Corinthians 15.19)

The complete good news, beginning in the first chapter of the Bible and ending in the last one, is that the God who created this present world supernaturally some six thousand years ago is going to make another one. He is going to create a new earth, and this time it will be a world that is free from decay, disease, death and everything else that has been the result of sin. He will live in this renewed earth himself in the person of his son Jesus Christ. Jesus will be king, and everyone who is willing to live under his kingship is invited to join him in that perfect kingdom to come. Here is how the Bible expresses this marvellous news:

> *...what we suffer now is nothing compared to the glory he will give us later. For all creation is waiting patiently and hopefully for that future day when God will resurrect his children. ... We, too, wait anxiously for that day when God will give us our full rights as his children, including the new bodies he has promised us – bodies that will never be sick again and will never die.* (Romans 8.18,19,23 TLB)

And here's how Jesus's favourite disciple, John, expressed the heart of that promise in the same Bible:

...God loved the world so much that he gave his only Son so that anyone who believes in him shall not perish but have eternal life.
(John 3.16 TLB)

Your choice, your decision

That verse in John's Gospel offers you and me a simple choice. When we die we can either perish or live for ever. By believing in Jesus you can come back to life in a new body, just as Jesus did when he rose from the dead. You can live with Jesus for ever in God's new creation and enjoy life in all its fullness, life as it was to begin with in the Garden of Eden, life as it was always intended to be.

Anyone who believes in him... The big question is, what does it mean to believe in Jesus?

When I was about seventeen years old I spent the first week of January with some other Scouts climbing mountains in Snowdonia. A man named Len was assigned to be our guide. Towards the end of the week he made an unexpected announcement. He wanted to take us up Snowdon, the highest mountain in Wales, not by one of the easier routes but over the dreaded Crib Goch ridge. The ridge is a knife-edge of rock a mile long with a steep drop of 1000 feet (300 metres) on each side of it. Even experienced climbers have fallen to their deaths from Crib Goch, for the ridge is only a few feet wide along the top and there is little to hold on to. Worse than that, we were going to cross it in the depths of winter, when it is covered in deep snow!

We didn't have to go with Len. We had a choice. We could go with him, or spend the day back in the safety and warmth of the hostel in Llanberis. But if we decided to trust Len to lead us safely over Crib Goch we would have to follow his instructions to the letter! Of course we all went with him. It was definitely frightening. Some of the Scouts even chose to crawl much of the way through the snow on their hands and knees rather than risk standing upright! But somehow we all managed to follow Len safely to the summit of Snowdon. It was a day none of us will ever forget!

Such an expedition would never be allowed in these days of enforced health and safety. It would have taken only one slip for someone to fall to his death that January. At the beginning of time it took Adam only one rebellious slip into sin to forfeit eternal life, both for himself and for the rest of the human race. (Romans 5.12) That's how serious sin is. All the troubles in this world are caused directly or indirectly by sin. And that causes God pain too. So this time he won't allow his coming kingdom to be spoilt by sin again. And that means there can be no sinners in it. (Revelation 21.27)

Therefore if you and I are going to live in the kingdom to come we must be changed. Only one person has ever lived without sin, and he is the only one who can enable us to do the same. Only one person has ever defeated death, and he is the only one who can enable us to defeat it too. Only one person has always lived and will always live, and he is the only one who can truly offer us everlasting life in all its fullness. The name of that one person is Jesus Christ. *"…there is salvation in no one else, for there is no other name under heaven given among men by which we must be saved."* (Acts 4.12)

Jesus is alive now. He is close to each one of us by his Spirit. He is close to you as you read this. To believe in him means to put your trust in him, just as we put our trust in Len. It means to put your trust in Jesus to save you from sin, to set you free from everything that would keep you out of the kingdom of God, and to give you eternal life. To put your trust in him means to be willing to follow his instructions implicitly, to put him first in everything you do, and to begin living now with him as your king, just as you will live when you come into his everlasting kingdom. Can you trust Jesus enough to surrender your life to him as both your saviour and your Lord? He once died for you. Will you live for him?

It's your decision. You can make it right now.

Begin a new life here and now

Find somewhere quiet where you can talk aloud to Jesus. He has been longing for this moment since before you were born. Use your own words, or say the following prayer if it expresses what's in your heart.

> *Dear Lord Jesus,*
>
> *I believe you are the Son of God. You know who I am. I realize that because of my sin I am under a death sentence. I am truly sorry for all the wrong things I have done and said and thought.* (If there's anything in particular on your conscience mention it.)
>
> *Please forgive me. With your help I now want to live the way you want me to and to fulfil the purpose you made me for.*
>
> *Lord Jesus,*

*I thank you very much that you died on
the cross so that I can be forgiven and set free
from sin to live for ever in your kingdom.*

*I now open the door of my life to you.
Please come in as my saviour and Lord, and
help me to live for you from this moment
onwards.*

Thank you, Lord Jesus.

Jesus said, *"All that the Father gives me will come to me;
and him who comes to me I will not cast out."* (John 6.37)
If you prayed like that and meant it you can be confident
that Jesus has accepted you and restored you to a right
relationship with the Father; that all your sins have been
forgiven and that you have the promise of everlasting life.

*'If we confess our sins, he is faithful and just,
and will forgive our sins and cleanse us from
all unrighteousness.'* (1 John 1.9)

*"…this is the will of my Father, that every one
who sees the Son and believes in him should
have eternal life; and I will raise him up at the
last day."* (John 6.40) What a great promise!

The Bible says that when we believe in Jesus to save us
and receive him as lord of our life we become a child of God.
(John 1.12) Here are some suggestions for your first steps as
God's new son or daughter.

(i) Make a permanent note of the date.

It's your new birthday! You'll want to remember this day in the future.

'*When someone becomes a Christian, he becomes a brand new person inside. He is not the same any more. A new life has begun!*' (2 Corinthians 5.17 TLB)

Making a note of the date is like inscribing it on the foundation stone of a new building.

(ii) <u>Tell someone what you have done.</u>

'*For if you tell others with your own mouth that Jesus Christ is your Lord and believe in your own heart that God has raised him from the dead, you will be saved.*' (Romans 10.9 TLB)

Telling someone is like cementing the foundation stone in place.

(iii) <u>Be baptized.</u>

'*Those who believe and are baptized will be saved.*' (Mark 16.16 TLB).

In the Bible baptism means being immersed in water by a church leader. It is a way of making public your decision to belong to Jesus, just as a wedding is a way of making public a decision to share one's life with someone else permanently. Baptism doesn't 'save' you, but it's how you show Jesus that you are willing to obey him, and how he shows you that your sins have been washed away and your new life with him has truly begun.

To be baptized you will have to find a church if you don't already belong to one. Churches can be big or small, formal or informal, dead or alive. A good local church will welcome you into God's family and help you to grow as a child of God. Do an Internet search for 'Lively church in Marshmere-under-Water / Little Grumbling / Dancing-by-the-Sea' or wherever you live, to find what's available. If several churches are listed, ask God to guide you and try visiting two or three of them on Sundays until you feel that you have found one that could become your spiritual home. Make sure they do proper baptisms!

Being baptized is like cementing other stones around you.

(iv) <u>Receive the Holy Spirit.</u>

Ask God to fill you with his Holy Spirit, or ask the church leaders at your baptism to pray that he will. *"…if even sinful persons like yourselves give children what they need, don't you realize that your heavenly Father will do at least as much, and give the Holy Spirit to those who ask for him?"* (Luke 11.13 TLB) You have to ask!

The Holy Spirit gives us the power to live as God wants us to. *'…those who follow after the Holy Spirit find themselves doing those things that please God.'* (Romans 8.5 TLB)

(v) <u>Find a mentor.</u>

If you already have a Christian friend ask if he or she would be willing to meet you on a regular basis for a while, to help you to learn how to follow Jesus. If you don't have such a friend, ask if there is someone in the church who would like to help you in this way.

(vi) <u>Talk to your heavenly Father each day.</u>
Find a quiet place to pray and follow the TSP 'teaspoon rule':

- *Thank* God for anything that comes to your mind.
- Tell him you are *sorry* for any way you've failed him and ask him to forgive you.
- Ask him *please* to help you and anyone else you know who is in need.

(vii) <u>Read the Bible.</u>
The Bible is like food for your spirit. It will enable you to grow into a strong Christian. If you don't have a Bible of your own you can download one as an app, or else you can buy an electronic or physical copy. There are different kinds of English translation. Search for 'Bibles for New Believers' for guidance on the translation that would best suit you.[77]

Annex 3 provides a useful list of Bible readings suitable for new Christians.

Ideally, set aside a time each day when you can read a passage of the Bible, think about it, and perhaps even make some notes on what you learn in a notebook or journal. My

---

[77] At the time of writing, one website providing guidance on the best Bibles for different kinds of people was eden.co.uk's Eden's Top 5 Bibles for New Believers.

wife and I read it together each morning in bed before we get up, and then we pray about what we have read as well as anything else that's on our minds.

Enjoy your new life as a citizen of heaven. And please introduce yourself to me when we meet in the resurrection!

If God has spoken to you through this book, please recommend it to your friends so that he can speak to them too. Encouraging reviews are always welcome on Amazon or other online booksellers, or on my own website, www. booksforlife.today.

And look out for my next book, *Z: Living in the Final Generation*!

Annex 1

Seven Days Of Expanding Time

In this annex I propose a theory which to some extent resolves the conflict between the Bible's statement that it took six literal days to create the universe and most scientists' insistence that it took 13.8 billion years. Personally I believe that the Bible's account of creation is literally true for the reasons I have explained, but if you still can't believe that God could make everything in six days of current time this might help you to believe the biblical account, provided that you have some knowledge of science and maths. I honestly don't know if my theory makes any sense to a physicist but I feel it's worth a shot, and it does seem possible to verify it to some extent, as you will read.

According to the big bang theory as I understand it, space expanded to accommodate all the material exploding from a single point of origin. In other words, space was created at the same time as matter was released. Initially space expanded very fast, but the rate of expansion decreased as time passed. However time is meaningless unless time was also created along with space. So let's suppose that time was also very compressed to start with and that it expanded rapidly at first and then gradually slowed down. What would that mean?

It would mean that in the beginning each second would take far less than a second now takes. So during one of our present seconds an enormous number of original seconds would initially have passed, enabling an awful lot to happen in that time. To us it would seem as though everything happened much faster than it does now.

Imagine another planet just like ours except that everything in it happened ten times as fast as it does on the earth. In a day of our time the inhabitants could achieve ten times as much as we can. On another planet where everything happened a hundred times as fast, the inhabitants could achieve a hundred times as much as we can in a day of our time.

I propose that initially time, like space, was infinitely compressed. Initially it expanded infinitely 'fast' but its rate of expansion decreased exponentially, until by the end of seven days of our current time it was more or less the same as time is now. This would mean that a great deal could have happened in the first day, and less and less as each day passed. Crucially, it would mean that in the time it takes for seven of our current 24-hour days to pass many, many more real days would have passed while the universe was being formed. In fact it could have taken 13.8 billion years of current time for the work to be completed. Hence creation could have taken place in six genuine days of current time, yet be 13.8 billion years old. Let's examine this idea more closely.

In Genesis we have the following sequence of creation:

Day 1 – light
Day 2 – the earth's atmosphere
Day 3 – separation of land and sea, and the creation of
        vegetation and trees
Day 4 – sun, moon and stars
Day 5 – fish and birds
Day 6 – animals, reptiles, etc., and people

This doesn't conform to any natural sequence – light before sun, and trees before stars! – so even with a theory of expanding time one cannot reconcile the Genesis account with any natural account of the creation of the world. However the order of events would appear more natural if the creation of the sun, moon and stars took place on day two rather than on day four, and the subsequent events took place a day later. If this was the order in which God originally said he had made things, the current order in Genesis might have come about through a lapse of memory on someone's part or it might have been changed on purpose by a scribe who believed that the earth was the centre of the universe and that it must therefore have been created before the sun, moon and stars were. If we make this single amendment to the current order of events in Genesis it appears to be much more natural.

Assuming a decreasing exponential rate of time expansion, the following formula will produce a decrease from 13.8 billion years for the age of the universe to 6000 years over seven days.

[6000 x (8 - *n*)]^7.53, where *n* is the day number

Hence, entering into the formula values of *n* from 1 to

7 for each day of creation we obtain the following apparent ages for each stage of creation:

1. 1.38E+10 – light, energy, space and time began 13.8 billion years ago
2. 4.32E+09 – sun, moon and stars were created 4.32 billion years ago
3. 1.09E+09 – Earth's atmosphere was created 1.09 billion years ago
4. 2.04E+08 – separation of land and sea, creation of vegetation and trees
5. 2.34E+07 – fish and birds
6. 1.11E+06 – animals, reptiles etc., and men
7. 6.00E+03 – God rested from his work of creation 6000 years ago

With these *calculated* ages for each stage of creation, the theory can be tested against the estimated ages of the listed events as commonly accepted. For instance the age assigned to the formation of the solar system is generally 4.53 billion years. That is very close to the 4.32 billion years predicted by the formula.

Other ages listed in Wikipedia's 'Timeline of evolutionary history of life' are as follows, in millions of years:

- fish   450 to 400
- land plants 360 to 220
- reptiles   225 to 100
- animals   170 to 4
- birds   110 to 25

- men   2 to 0.25.

Table A.1 compares the age of each stage of creation as calculated by my formula with its generally accepted age. With the exception of fish the two sets of data match remarkably closely.

Table A.1: Comparison of calculated and accepted dates for the formation of the world

Stage		Years ago		Original
n	Description	Wikipedia article on the evolutionary history of life	Predicted by formula $6000 \times (8 - n)^{7.527}$	day number in Genesis
1	'Big bang'	13.8 billion	13.8 billion[a]	1[b]
2	Solar system	4530 million	4320 million	4
3	Earth's atmosphere	4500 to 1000 million[c]	1090 million	2
4	Vegetation and trees	360 to 35 million	204 million	3
5	Birds	110 to 25 million	23.4 million	5
6	Reptiles, animals and man	225 to 0.25 million	1.11 million	6
7	God rested	n/a	6000	7
3.5[d]	*Fish*	*450 to 400 million*	*495 million*	5

[a] Matched to scientific estimate, so not predicted.
[b] Equating "Let there be light!" with the big bang.
[c] 4500 million first atmosphere, 1000 million formation of oxygen.
[d] In order to match the evolutionary date given to fish, we have to assume that fish were created midway between days three and four, instead of on day five as the Bible says.

Apart from the fish date, my predicted dates based on a revised order of events in Genesis match the generally accepted scientific dates pretty well. They match very well indeed the scientific dates for the cosmological events that preceded the supposed emergence of life. And as I explained in Chapter 5, the dates commonly assigned to the emergence of various life forms are based on very dubious evidence. If palaeontologists were to announce in the future that the first fish appeared much later than they originally thought, in fact at much the same time as birds, it would add immense credence to my little theory and perhaps even make me famous!

Personally I take the Bible's account of creation at its face value, so I'm not actually convinced that my theory is true. The universe could only have been created supernaturally, as I explained in my book *Z: The Final Generation*, and if God created it supernaturally then he could have done it in any period of time he chose, even instantaneously.

Nevertheless, it would be very nice if my little theory were true. It would explain why I never seem to achieve so much in a day as I used to. It's not because I am growing old: it's because time is still expanding!

Annex 2

Jews On Earth And Gentiles In Heaven?

There is a belief sincerely held by some Christians that Jewish believers in Christ and some of the very first non-Jewish believers will eventually live on the new earth, while all other non-Jewish believers will live in heaven. The idea that Gentile (non-Jewish) believers will live with Christ in heavenly places rather than on earth is based on Ephesians 2.4-7, as I explained in Chapter 10.

It's not within the scope of this book to explain why they believe that Jews and Gentiles will be treated differently, but what I want to do here is explain why I can't accept such a belief.

- It seems to contradict everything Paul wrote in the rest of Ephesians chapter 2. In Christ, he wrote, Jews and Gentiles have been made one; they are fellow citizens and they are joined together into a holy temple in the Lord. How can any of this be true if Jewish believers are going to live on the earth while Gentile believers live in heaven?

- In Ephesians chapter 4 Paul goes even further. *'There is one body and one Spirit, just as you were called to the one hope that belongs to your call...'* How can Jewish and Gentile believers have one and the same hope if some of them hope to live on the earth and the others hope to live in heaven? Or how can they be one body if it is split into two halves?

- In Galatians 3.28,29 Paul tells his readers, '*There is neither Jew nor Greek, there is neither slave nor free, there is neither male nor female; for you are all one in Christ Jesus. And if you are Christ's, then you are Abraham's offspring, heirs according to the promise.*' In other words God makes no distinction between Jews and non-Jews who believe in Jesus Christ, any more than he distinguishes between slave and free, male and female.

- There were Jewish believers in the church at Ephesus to which Paul was writing. (See Acts 19.1) So when he wrote that God 'made us sit with him in the heavenly places in Christ Jesus' the 'us' must have included Jewish readers as well as the Gentile ones. If this really means that the destiny of believers is to live in heaven it must include Jewish Christians too.

- As we saw in Chapter 10, the Bible clearly teaches that the Lord Jesus will return to the earth to reign. '*On that day his feet shall stand on the Mount of Olives which lies before Jerusalem on the east... Then the Lord your God will come, and all the holy ones with him. ... And the Lord will become king over all the earth...*' (Zechariah 14.4,5,9) If Jesus is going to reign on the earth in the age to come, how can Gentile believers not be on the earth yet remain seated with him in heaven?

- The belief that Gentile Christians will be privileged to spend eternity in heavenly places with Christ, while Peter and Paul and the rest of Christ's *Jewish* apostles will have to stay down here on the earth, can only appear to be racist, however sound may be the reasons for such a belief. I would be most uncomfortable at the idea that as a Gentile believer I shall have a more privileged position than Christ's first apostles.
- Revelation 5.9,10 says that Jesus has ransomed men 'from *every* tribe and tongue and people and nation', i.e. both Jews and Gentiles. He has 'made them a kingdom' and 'they shall reign *on earth*'. That is about the future ('they shall reign') and it means that in the future all resurrected believers in Jesus will live on the earth.

As believers in Jesus Christ as saviour we all share in one, single, glorious hope, whether we are Jews or Gentiles, male or female, rich or poor. Guaranteed by the promises of Jesus and by the reality of his own resurrection from the dead, we shall live together with him on a new earth. He will rule over a worldwide kingdom in which sin and all its horrible consequences will be replaced by unity, love, truth, justice, peace and unimaginable joy for ever and ever. What a glorious hope we have!

Annex 3

Fifty-Day Bible Reading Plan

Reproduced by permission of Shoreline Community Church, Monterey, California.

By now you must have realized that a reference like 'Luke 4.14-44' means the book of Luke, chapter 4, verses 14 to 44. At the front of any Bible you'll find a page index to the various books in it.

The Story of the Christian Faith (New Testament)

Day 1. Luke chapters 1 & 2: The birth of Jesus

Day 2. John 1.1-18: The identity of Jesus

Day 3. Luke 4.14-44: Jesus begins his ministry

Day 4. Matthew 5 & 6: The core of Jesus's teachings

Day 5. John 3: God's love for the world

Day 6. John 5: Jesus's miracles and authority

Day 7. John 11: Jesus's power over death

Day 8. John 15: The Christian life defined

Day 9. Matthew 26 & 27: The arrest and crucifixion of Jesus

Day 10. John 20 & Luke 24: The resurrection of Jesus and his ascension

Day 11. Acts 2: The coming of the Holy Spirit

Day 12. Acts 9.16-19: The conversion of Saul and his ministry

Day 13. Acts 26: Paul's defence of the Christian faith

Day 14. Romans 3: Justification by faith alone

Day 15. Romans 7 & 8: The battle with sin, and life in the Spirit

Day 16. 1 Corinthians 13, Ephesians 5: The way of love

Day 17. 1 Corinthians 15: The power of the resurrection

Day 18. Galatians 5, Ephesians 4: Freedom and unity in Christ

Day 19. Ephesians 6: The whole armour of God

Day 20. Philippians 1.18 to 2.18: Christ's example

Day 21. Colossians 3.1-17: Putting on the new self

Day 22. Hebrews 4.14 to 5.10: Jesus the great high priest

Day 23. James 1 & 1 Peter 1: Pure religion

Day 24. 1 John 4.7-21: God is love

Day 25. Revelation 21 & 22: The new heaven and earth.

Old Testament survey

Day 26. Genesis 1.1 to 3.19: The creation and fall of humanity

Day 27. Genesis 12; 28.10-15; 32.22-28: God calls a people his own

Day 28. Genesis 37; 39 to 46: The story of Joseph

Day 29. Exodus 1 to 6: The call of Moses

Day 30. Exodus 7 to 14: Moses and Pharaoh

Day 31. Exodus 19.1 to 20.2: The Ten Commandments

Day 50. Malachi 1 to 4: Final words of the Old Testament.

Further help can be found in *Every Day with Jesus for New Christians*, published by the Crusade for World Revival as a small paperback and as an e-book.

Other books by the same author

Z: The Final Generation. Biblical prophecy reveals the date of Christ's return.
(Book 1 in the series)
Published by WestBow Press in 2018
    ISBN: 978-1-9736-3021-0 (sc)
    ISBN: 978-1-9736-3020-3 (e)
This book examines the evidence for God's existence, exposes the fallacies of the generally accepted theories about the origin of the universe and life on Earth, and explains how the Bible's account of a relatively recent creation can be squared with scientific measurements of a much greater age. It goes on to demonstrate how biblical prophecy and other evidence point inexorably to a date for Christ's return around the year 2033.
Available from www.booksforlife.today and through all good booksellers.

Twenty-first Century Nutrition and Family Health
Published by New Generation Publishing in 2015.
    ISBN: 978-1-78507-177-5
    ASIN: B00SRDI34M
This important book explains what is wrong with current recommendations for healthy eating and provides clear guidance on a truly healthy diet and lifestyle. It is supported by references to over 500 peer-reviewed scientific papers and similar publications. The author's wife was taken off thirteen years of medication for Type 2 diabetes when the recommended diet corrected her blood sugar level. Having adopted both the diet and the recommended exercise regime, the author at the age of 70 climbed all sixteen peaks in Snowdonia over 3000 feet high in 24 hours.
Available from www.booksforlife.today.

In preparation

Z: Living in the Final Generation. Preparing for Christ's imminent return.

Printed in the United States
By Bookmasters